Poems and Spoken Word Pieces

Written By:
Howard McAfee

PUBLISHED BY:
ONNEY PUBLISHING AND PERFORMANCES INC

Copyright © 2017
Howard McAfee

ISBN-13: 978-0-9973128-3-6
ISBN-10: 0-9973128-3-1
LCCN: 2017905335

Cover Designed By:
Howard McAfee.

Onney Publishing & Performances, Inc.
P.O. Box 309
Missouri City, Texas 77584
www.onney.net

RIGHTS RESERVED:

Without limiting the rights under the copyright reserved above, no part of this publication may be reproduced, stored in or introduced into a retrieval system, or transmitted in any form or by any means (electronic, mechanical, photocopying, recording or otherwise), without prior written permission of both the copyright owner or the above publisher of this book.

PUBLISHERS NOTE:

The scanning, uploading and distribution of this book via the Internet or via any other means without the permission of the publisher is illegal and punishable by law. Please purchase only authorized electronic editions, and do not participate in or encourage electronic editions, and do not participate in or encourage electronic piracy of copyrighted materials. Your support of the author's rights is appreciated.

"One of my greatest fears is to be forgotten or lost in memory. One of my greatest gifts is my daughter. So, using a great gift, I dedicate a few lost memories, good and bad, to my greatest gift of all...Marlee."

<u>Ol' Skool.</u>

Introduction

"Hashtag Poet Ol Skool" is sort of like a jigsaw puzzle. Imagine looking through a kaleidoscope into the calm eye of the storm with cataracts and a sty that's doubled, and Visine barely soothes what shouldn't be dry, but just adds more debris into the struggle.

So, I will tell you now that there will never be any muzzle on my thoughts. My speech is graffiti and I see in caligraphy to make you hear screaming undertones of what's written in between the lines of rhymes that can't be caught.

So when chaos is sought, this is my peace be still. There is no need for you to try to steal a piece of me because I'm handing it you in this paper platter. My flesh bleeds ink. This is mind over black matter. What you see isn't what you think, so when blinded by truth, the lies will shatter.

With mischievous laughter, this is the way I chose to die with a hashtag. If you believe in the mind, the body will soon follow, even if the words are doomed, hollowed and wrapped in at trash bag.

They say if you want to hide anything from black folks put it in a book. But if knowledge about me is what you seek and you can't hear it from those who speak, only within the pages is where you find the words and wisdom of what you look.

Slightly more than a mental crook, I am a man, a father, a friend with a daughter. A poet, a writer, a worker, a fighter. I am a man that is known to wear many hats that can use many tools. I am black power, hidden behind my own cool.

This is my hashtag. I am Ol' Skool.

Table of Contents

Conversation Kills I	1
Conversation Kills II	3
Conversation Kills III	5
Conversation Kills IV	7
Conversation Kills V	9
Conversation Kills VI	11
Conversation Kills VII	13
Conversation Kills VIII	15
Conversation Kills IX	17
Conversation Kills X	19
Black Rage	21
Dispel the Myth	23
Don't March for Me	25
Educate Yourself	27
Faith without Works	29
Forgiveness	31
Ghetto Evolution	32
I Am Black Power	35
If You Knew Better	37
Harsh Reality	39
Inspiration	41
Lethal	43
One Tear Ain't Crying	45
Pissed Off Peddler	47
Racial Injustice	49
RIPTM	51
Self Made Man	52
Sick and Tired	54
Step Your Game Up	56
Strength Of A Black Woman	58
Hear Them Cry	61
The New	63
The Struggle	65
Time of Hate	68
Untitled	70
What's Sexy	72

Living Proof	74
Ambush	76
Dreamless Death	78
Emotions Unheard Of	80
Escape	82
Frustration	83
Heaven Or Hell	84
Hold My Hand	85
Magic Mirror	86
Ol' Skool's Blues	87
Prisoner	90
Questioning Love	91
Reflection	92
Sabotage	93
Scrambled Thoughts	95
Shackled	96
Solitary Entrapment	98
Spiritually Dehydrated	100
Suicide	101
The Glass Eye	102
Time Will Heal	104
To Whom It May Concern	105
Unheard Cries	106
Message to my Daughter	107
Enough	109
For Better or Worse	111
For Momma	115
From A Father	117
Ghost of The Ghetto	120
Grandma's Hands	122
Marlee	124
Pain and Sin	125
Sunday Morning	127
Temper Tantrum	129
True Story	133
Brainstorming	134
Dear Departed	136

Forgive me...	137
Gypsy Eyes	138
Never	140
On My Mind	142
Saying Goodbye	143
Thank You	144
Unfinished Business	145
Battle Ground	147
Bitch's Advocate	149
Bona-fied Beast	151
Crack Cocaine	153
Cut Throat	156
Don't Judge Me	158
Don't Judge Me Again	160
Grand Slam	162
I Ain't Welcome	164
Kryptonite	166
Lyrical Punishment	168
Male Bash	170
Ol Skool	173
On the Rag	175
Power Of My Words	176
Reason To Hate Me	179
Heathenism	181
Trifling Hoes	183
Truth and Bullshit	185
Won't Be Defeated	187
A Long Walk	189
Dominance	190
Got That Wood	192
Keep it on the Hush	193
Reading is Fundamental	195
Rehabilitation	206

Conversation Kills I
Drug Addict

One good got damn hit was all it took is what she told me. And I'll be the first to admit I've sucked dicks, licked splits, and stolen shit just so another hit could console me.

She said, Ol' Skool I need someone to hold me and truly understand my pain. All I could do was listen as the words trembled from her dry lips as she spoke them in vain.

Rubbing the tracks in her own veins she said, I even used to run around in the stormy rain to the nearest dope man just for a five dollar bump. It just kept calling my name and was like jumping on the Titanic for that last ride and thrill even though I knew it had sunk.

And I'll be the first to tell you she used to have it all. I told her you never get what you deserve until you've earned it and you never realize what you had till it's good and gone. She laughed and said Ol' Skool, but it's an addiction. You never know what you've been missing till it arrives on your door step when you're alone at home.

I didn't choose this life, it's been a life chosen for me to live. Just like it wasn't Adam's choice for Eve to be made from his rib.

In these streets it's give and take. I've been beaten and raped. I know where I come from and where I've been around here. She said even though I don't know where I'm going any road I take even if I get lost on the way is bound to get me there.

I can't afford to continue or stop doing what I do because it's an addiction that I can not beat. And no one in this fucking world can judge me or hold a grudge against me because we all have one it's just that my addiction is in the streets.

I don't gamble or drink, and don't care too much for sex but even the great Rick James knew that cocaine is a powerful drug. Then I told her I can't help nobody that won't help themselves. And she told me with a straight face Ol Skool, that doesn't mean you have to take away all your love.

Life is a game of push and shove so if I rub you the wrong way forgiveness is all that I ask. I had a laid-off father that beat me, a part time mother that would leave me, with full time bullshit to deceive me, but even I was able to forgive their ass.

So I asked her, how long did that forgiveness last, since it was ghosts from the past because you get what you inspect out of life not what you expect. You have to play the cards you're dealt to the best of your ability; you just can't ask the dealer to reshuffle the deck.

Then she told me yeah, that's true. But how do I forgive myself for a life long regret. I lost my self-respect. Now I don't know what to do next.

And if that ain't some shit that's just plain worthless. Of all the itching I've had for another hit, what I've just told is barely scraping the surface.

My life keeps me cursing because I can't control this evil demon living within me. I've even sold a hot piece of pussy for a good bump and didn't care if the nigga's semen leaked all in me.

I can't explain the feeling when you wrap your lips around that glass dick and take that, hit that shit quick with that blue flame and no shame to puff slowly so it can control you and be inhaled into your brain.

And because of that pain I've been a thief in the night, living the un-living life that death won't even accept me into. Sometimes I feel like the living dead, that everyday living life dread when the demon gets all in you.

I've been trying to get this monkey off of my back since the first time. Ol' Skool, but I'm telling you, it's so hard to get that monkey off of your back when that monkey is still on your mind.

I just don't know what to do. For some reason I just can't help myself. Then I told her whether that be the case or not, the story you just told just helped someone else.

Don't judge a book by its cover. You never know what you can learn from the next sister or brother and what they've been through so we should all find a way to at least respect one another.

Love is like no other and is stronger than any addiction. Hell... love is the one that the next person may be missing.

You should always try to keep a hand on the times. And never let the time get a hand on you.

Conversation Kills II
Drug Dealer

I am only a product if my environment is what he'd always tell me. From crack rock to cocaine to the shit that goes in your veins, even the instruments are what he tried to sell me.

He said, Ol' Skool I just really need someone to help me and truly understand my pain. And all I could do was listen as those words would creep from behind his gold and diamond teeth as he spoke them in vain.

Tugging on the charm from the chain round his neck, he said, I've even sold drugs in exchange for sex or other types of favors. If you want it, I got it, if I ain't got it, I'mma get it. Whatever you need, player, like Baskin Robbins, I got 31 flavors.

Then I asked him when was the last time he spoke to his savior because this type of behavior is not what the Lord has planned for you. Little boys and girls sit up and watch you sell boy and girl to another man or two after you have rocked up a gram or two.

Then he said I don't give a damn what you think, I do what I have to do, to avoid the struggle. If dope dealing was just drug dealing and no feelings, I'd be a lost lamb hustling in a land with no appealing or muscle.

And since it gives me so much access to a world of free living, I laugh at the thought of giving up and quitting. As a matter of fact you should switch to my lane and change your way of living.

And that's when I told him with so much feeling, but you're killing your own people. You won't sell it to your mother or your brother, but you'd sell your homeboy down the street some shit that would keep him closer to a casket and steeple from the end of a drastic needle.

Then he said he would get past his people. He was born into struggle, raised to scuffle and will die in the hustle because it seems as if his life has been planned. I then told him, why would you let plans make you? You have to makes plans yourself to have a better hustle so you can keep the upper hand.

That way you can make a couple of grand the right way and wouldn't have to worry about the police being on your ass. Cooking soft and selling hard then bleeding the block and boulevard; I'm telling you, jail is not the best way for time to pass.

Your way of life can't and has never lasted for anyone forever. The cocoa leaf has been extracted since the 1860's and crack has been cooked since the early 80's, but no man has ever lived a flawless life selling cocaine and crack forever.

I mean, whether sniffed, shot up, or smoked, even the nigga that sold the dope is bound to choke and is headed down the wrong path. And many may hold a grudge against you, but it's said that only God can judge you, so trust me, you will feel the unjust power of His strong wrath.

How long really are you going to let this sad song last, being a dope dealer? Then he said he sells hopes and dreams to buy him things that bling, as if he was a pope, but true to it and so realer.

He said this is all I've ever done and this is all that I know. It's the only way I know how to provide for a lifestyle of flash and front to show.

Then I told him, there is a vast difference between a man that can't read and a man that will not. It's your choice to be ignorant and stupid; living the story of your own life and not even knowing the real plot.

I told told him, it's not over for you; you still got time to turn your life around to a life of good. The last time I went to jail, I told all of my people to leave me there. That's the only way I will truly learn and get the point understood.

If they keep pulling me out of the water, I would never know what drowning feels like. But you're drowning now, so I want to help save you from a confined and concealed life.

Because the overall real price to pay for your type of life today is either behind bars or six feet underground. Slow singing and flower bringing will be the only sounds floating throughout the town.

Then he thought for a moment as if he was feeling the words I spoke. Then another man approached us asked for some dope. He smiled at me and then sold him some shit that would make him choke.

He said I can never stop or go broke as long as the demand is high for getting high and the supply is low. And as soon as he walked away, he was stopped by the police and the reason why, you already know.

The guy he sold that blow to was an undercover. So he just passed up his last chance to start a new way of life and become another.

Conversation Kills III
The Prostitute

She said; let a bitch pimp her own pussy. And I'm telling you that, Ol' Skool, from the bottom of my heart. Because it ain't a man on God's green earth that a woman hasn't taught.

Everyday, life is sold, bullshitted, then bought so why am I hated, why can't I do the same? I ain't proud of this shit I do, why do you think I ran away with an alias name to a life of shame?

Ol' Skool, I just can't escape the pain. I was born to trouble, raised to hustle, and am going to die living the struggle because that's all about life that I know. And it ain't no puzzle, because no big huddle of people will ever care or cry one drop of a puddle if I die as long as I live in the lie and continue to be the star of my own show.

So slander my name and call me a hoe, but, Ol' Skool, I'm what you would call a professional woman of leisure. That's when I spoke up and asked her, how you can go about living your life selling your ass for cash, being a professional dick pleaser?

Doesn't that shit make you sick easier knowing that you are the primary prey to most sexual predators, women and men? And that's when she said, but it's all I know. The world is and has been a battlefield from within and my life has been on a gurney throughout my whole journey of sin.

Baby, boy, my life isn't that different from some of my women friends in the clubs. I mean let's be real, most won't even begin to deal with a man unless he's big spending and pockets are showing love.

Only difference is, is that I am upfront and willing to use my chocolate glove to go to the end to get it. And I admit it, I've turned tricks, sucked dick and licked splits, the same shit other women do for gifts or money, just to spend it.

Whether some of those men give it or not is the least of my worries. And addiction is another one of the problems, no one can help solve'em, but even that's just one of my many stories.

Ol' Skool, sometimes you got to do what you hate to do in order to do what you want to. Then I told her, yeah that's true, but you have to understand that those things you may want, you might not need and could later in life haunt you.

You have to give the best of yourself in order to receive the best. In the Bible, Kane killed Abel because of his triumph and success after giving his best. Then, the jealous possessed Kane was punished, and ostracized from the land he worked and loved, away from the rest.

If you are going to give yourself to someone, why not give them the best of you? She said I hear you… And I know it's sinful, but every time the wind blows and I peer through that half-open window the sin goes right out with the breeze. And sometimes after staring into the eyes of faceless men, I've been kidnapped, beaten, and raped even after my community service of being on my knees.

So why won't you stop, I then asked. It's not that easy, she shot back. I'm going to die in these streets, but for you I'll always be around. I've been doing this for fifteen-plus years. And of all the shit I've been through, now, just being broke is one of my greatest fears.

And when she released a tear, I knew she was really hurting. How could her life escalate so far? When she started off, she was just in the clubs playing and flirting.

Momma taught her but daddy left her, and I guess that's why the streets kept her. Like they say, birds of a feather flock together. She had dreams of being queen of the castle, but instead became queen of the streets and the hustle, and all those that didn't know any better.

She was just like any other woman in cold weather learning how to live in a fast-paced world that wouldn't stand still. And a week after that conversation we had, she had been stabbed seven times in the chest and killed.

Against her will, she was off duty at a club. And the killer was a drunken man that bought her a few drinks that she accepted even though she knew she had no plans on showing him any love.

Watch who you try to play for their cash. You never know who is big spending, but the price may cost you your ass, and that breath you take may be your last.

Conversation Kills IV
Bitter Black Woman

What in the fuck did I ever do to deserve this shit? I gave him every part of me and my being that there is to give. Love, salvation, honor, affection, trust, faith; everything that Adam would've needed for Eve to complete his other side and soul to keep him safe; I was his missing rib.

But still, I got fucked over in the process. I mean, I loved him...but like a fool I was blinded by a false progress.

I guess I just got what I deserved. And that's when I stopped her in her tracks to calm down her wrath and told her, baby you did nothing. He was the one with the nerve.

He couldn't observe the strength of your loving ways and serve you with a hope for better days. She said, I never asked for him to change. I just wanted him to curve his love and affection in my direction, and rearrange that path in a way for it to stay.

But, I guess that's what I get on any day for dealing with these sorry ass niggas. Then I told her, you can't say that. He wasn't sorry when you met him, remember. He was the soul icon of a loving figure.

You have to be a bigger woman than that. Maybe he just wasn't ready for the life that you had planned. You got with him when he was with another. What made you so sure that he would just quit what he's been doing and be your man?

You knew what the deal was before the two of you got together; a friendly fuck, you just got your feeling involved. Then she snapped at me quick and said all men ain't shit, all of you mother fuckers are just dogs.

I then told her, naw, you just got it in your mind that your prime pussy meat can make any man change, but baby let me tell you, from a pussy he came. Only pain can make a man change his ways as long as he wants the same.

So I am to blame, she said. Is that what you are trying to tell me? I know the game can't be told; only sold, Ol' Skool, so sell me what I need to know to help me.

I'm so hurt and scorned from a life that my own ways have dealt me that I just don't know what to do. I've slashed tires, keyed cars, and put sugar in tanks. And don't get me wrong it made me feel a whole lot better, but that's not the entire truth.

Ol' Skool, I admire you because you are the only one I know that will break it down. Then I told her with a straight face, baby, if you ever done that shit to me, I'd do the same shit he done and slapped your ass around.

Baby, you can never beat a man at his own hustle in his own town or double cross a snake from the back. They say actions speak louder than words, but that doesn't mean your words are silent and have no impact.

The Bible says the power of life and death is lies with your tongue, and if you have enough faith in a mustard seed, you can move mountains. You say all of this shit about him, but really the both of you drink from the same fountain.

You can't blame or be mad at him because he followed the rules and regulations. He was good to you like he was supposed to do, but it's really your fault that you got caught up in the stipulations.

But he said he was done playing those games, is what she then told me. He said that he wanted to be the only one to hold me.

And I shot back coldly, how you know he didn't tell the same thing to his ex when they got together? Baby, you got to be true to it, not new to it, you can't be in the middle of the summer and let a nigga sell you a sweater.

Whatever the case may be, I know that women love deeper than men. That's a known fact. So if you are playing the game, play it to the fullest, don't pretend or act, knowing there's a chance you can get stabbed in the back.

But I can tell you one thing, I know for a fact that he's hurting too, because women have always had all the power. Women can get wet with no water, make things harder without touch, bleed with no injury, make niggas eat without cooking, and can make a minute seem like an hour.

So the next time you try to get sour over a man because you feel you got fucked. Check yourself and look in the mirror before you go out with the mission to change a man's luck.

Conversation Kills V
The Convict

I was born and destined to be a known felon is what he told me. And I admit, I've shed tears over childhood fears, but truth is no-one was ever there through the years to hold me.

This is what life has always shown me, so fuck it I took a route on the first thing smoking. And even though the air had me choking, I was like Snipes and Harrelson because the money train was always open.

And I had that token, so whoever had a problem, fuck 'em, I couldn't help solve them, there's nothing to compromise. Then I told him, yeah, but you have to remember that just about everyone has lived lies and the same things that can make you laugh are the same things that can make you cry.

You have to try to figure out a better way to live a spiritual life away from crime, violence, and 'drug sells'. Because the only difference between a man that's free and a man in jail is the fact that some just got caught on the way to heaven, taking a short cut through hell.

Then he pressed his forehead to the two and a half thick glass as if he wanted to yell and said, all my life I've been surrounded by violence. I was a prisoner of my own fears before I was sentenced the years. I even became shaken up by total silence.

I never wanted to try this, but since I can't part from here I keep something sharp under my pillow next to my heart in fear. On the outside, you can get away, but on the inside, you're here to stay and no-one better ever see you bitch up on any day and shed a tear.

I didn't want this way of life, the streets chose me. I'm a product of the struggle. I'm what anyone would say I'm supposed to be.

I was just doing me, and if doing me fucked someone in the process...I could really care less that they got fucked from my personal progress.

I was born in the gutter with no bread and butter and a part time mother who'd smother her love on another brother. I had to handle the struggle the best way I knew how in between the clutter to find my own way out from under the cover.

Then I uttered something that stopped him dead in his tracks. My nigga, I went and came from the same bullshit you were drug through in life. So the shit you just said is no excuse for that.

I know what it feels like to be treated like a doormat or even see your own sister pushed and shoved or even beaten. I know what it feels like to have your mother steal from your piggy bank in stormy rain for a quick fix or lived in a house where no one was eating.

My people have been in and out of jail. I've lived through and prevailed from what some folks would call hell.

I've had to open tons of mail from my mother just because she couldn't make bail. I've had to deal with a sperm donor who ain't worth a crack bitch's wicked and crooked spell in hell.

I've even been trapped behind the chipped painted bricks and cold steel of a locked cell. I know what it's like to have the Jaws of Life enclose on you like the inside of a clam's shell.

So don't give me this bullshit about how a fucked up life held you down. Then he sat there in total silence, shocked by my sudden science with his head to the ground.

He looked up to me and said pound for pound I'm the number one prize fighter in the joint. And no-one has ever had the nuts to break it down in that way to prove their point.

He says I can respect a man that will show that passion. Then I told him, I'm just trying to show you a way from all of this negative action.

A fork in the road presents an opportunity and possibility for God to show himself to you to let you know who you are. I told him this is that fork. Although many battles have been lost, this is your chance to win the war.

I know it's hard to reinvent yourself from who you are, giving yourself advice on unfamiliar territory, mapping uncharted waters. But you are a child of the Lord. He has never turned his back and let down any of His sons or daughters.

And after I said that, my jail visit was over. And about six months later, he was up for parole and got out; and since then he's been winning the war as his own spiritual soldier.

Conversation Kills VI
The Unborn Child

"Please, mamma, stop, why you are doing this to me? Why are you constantly trying to steal my life away? I want to live." An unborn child's words go unheard because its mother has the ability to give the gift of life but for some reason that's just a gift in life she doesn't want to give.

"Please, just give me a chance at life then I wouldn't even mind if you just gave me away if things were really getting hard. If I really wanted to die I'd just punish myself and commit suicide by choking myself with this umbilical cord."

"I promise to you I won't be bad. I'll do anything you say and be one of the good kids. They say it's survival of the fittest so all I ask is the chance of life to be physically fit to prove this."

It's not that the mother doesn't want kids. The bad thing is that the fact of the matter is its mother was beaten and raped against her will so that's how her decision really came to this.

Brutalized and left for dead, this woman became a victim of hardship and circumstance. She tried to put up a decent fight but from the very beginning she really had no chance.

A pissed off woman and a woman scorned create symptoms of an emotional distress where there is really no antidote to be seeking. They say what doesn't kill you makes you stronger but isn't it logical if you kill what's a part of you, you really make yourself weaker.

Abortion is a tough decision that truly lies upon the mind of the woman. So how do you choose between life or death of what's a part of you even if it's from a part of a life that violated the life you knew before the growing of the life in the pits stomach.

"This is my plea to you, so I'm begging you because I know my daddy did you wrong. I can even feel the tears you cry sometimes when you ball up in the corner when you're alone at home."

But would you listen if you knew that those tears were derived from the fears of a rapists' clone that lie within that innocent crawling to the surface from the soul of a woman that was done completely wrong?

"How can I truly make you understand that I can't be held accountable for the actions of a sexual predator that raped you? All I want is the chance at life. If you gave me away, later in life I would understand and wouldn't even hate you."

But even the Bible says we should cry when children are born and rejoice when they're deceased. A child is born from sin into a world of sin suffers more in life than when it dies and is released into a world of total peace.

"All I want is a chance at life. A first kiss. A good fight. Perhaps, even a slow dance at my high school prom one night. Please hear me out. Because I'm not misunderstanding you. Actually, I'm asking you for a favor. You can even call it a lifesaver."

So what would you choose when there's nothing left... life for an innocent child conceived completely from sin, or death for a life to completely live free in the end?

To all women and men in here I ask if this happened to you and heard that voice. Do you think you could unregrettably with no guilty conscious make that choice? I think not.

Conversation Kills VII
The Pimp

If nothing else sells in this world, believe me, Ol' Skool, when I tell you, you can have any girl, because pussy will sell. Even in a cold depressed world of hate and no love, that hot chocolate glove will still be sought and bought, whether on the streets or in mud.

Even if a man could get it in the mail, a convict in a jail cell would spend his last on a piece of ass instead of commissary. This is supply and demand and since you can't get high off your on supply, the demand is steady rising high. I sell pussy because it's necessary.

He said, and these bitches better pay me and make that money. Then I laughed at him like it was funny and said how can you honestly treat women this way? All women are queens of the castle, not the hustle, so why do you exploit their sexual muscles for pay?

He then said, well, what can I say; I really don't know how I got here, but there are no other feelings to compare. From a pussy I came, so I guess that why I don't want to leave the game. I chose to stay there.

Ol' Skool, it may not seem fair, but you are sharing your words to a gamer. I'm not a joker. If you put a bad bitch in front of me, I'm telling you, I'm guaranteed to work and poke her.

I got the best hand at the table and that maybe the main reason I'm playing. I'm sitting in the best seat in the house, so you can probably figure out why I'm staying.

I then shot back, but don't you care for any of these women and who they're laying with. He then said, I wouldn't give a good fuck who they with as long as they're making my money and paying it.

Ol' Skool, you got to understand that just the gift of gab alone can persuade a king's daughter. And these girls are young, misguided and undecided; I'm just trying to make their life a little easier than harder.

He said, Ol' Skool, just like water, I provide a service to the community. Just like the police I sometimes pay, I am here to stay and it's like I have been granted legal immunity.

I'm soon to be known as one of the greatest. And whether you hate this or not, there will always be a willing cock wanting a shaved kiss and will pay that big buck for a lil' suck and fuck from the tasteless.

I appreciate the nice word, but I'm like Iceberg and will bleed a bitch dry. I could be worse. I *could* be selling the type of shit that would make the blood fry.

Ol' Skool, I've seen it all. Niggas be more faithful and real to their side bitch, than their main bitch, and main bitches are more worried about a side bitch than taking care of her main bitch duties. Tricks buy coochie that ain't worth shit like stripper booty, and real women give grade "A" pussy away for free and will even make homemade movies.

What you see as a priceless beauty I see as the nicest booty that comes with a price to be paid. And since we know it's nice to be laid, I'll put a dollar amount on that ass until it's twice in the grave.

This has been the life that's been paved for me since I was a young boy, playing Pick-up Sticks. My mother turned tricks for money or a quick fix and my father stole shit and sold it for quick licks, so I was destined for these slick schemes to get rich.

I don't give a fuck about a trick bitch with two sets of deceiving lips as long as they give me monetary gifts after receiving tips. He said, and there's nothing like a thoroughbred chick with thick thighs, bedroom eyes, and conceiving hips.

What's understood shouldn't have to be explained. I know it's wrong, but my brain has already been trained to drain these women to the soul like a useless picture in an antique frame.

I then told him, yea…but one day you may hang for what you're doing. He laughed and said yea…that's probably true… but I'll still be above you from the money from screwing.

I swallowed my pride and will die chewing on this shit until that reaper from hell is sent. He said Ol' Skool, just tell the world when I've paid up my rent, from a pussy I came…and from a pussy I went.

Conversation Kills VIII
Gangster

Dig this here, my nigga. I've been shot up and shot down, even when my finger was nowhere near the trigger, so don't sell me some wolf ticket about how I should be bigger than the next figure with plex, just tripping because I'm from another set. It's real in the field, so you can bet that I'm first with nine left to go in the chamber to check a hater in danger who's **talking** shit out of context.

He said, Ol' Skool, I was born and bred into this life of strife, and even at home I had to fight most nights for my rights. With no father, I already felt abandoned, so I left home, at random, when things went wrong and weren't right because sometimes it felt better to get away from all the barking and the ferocious bites.

So, I got dead in his view of sight and said, so…what's your point. You're just singing the same old sad song I hear from everyone else that's been locked up in the joint.

Why would you even allow or keeping blaming your past to keep carrying your ass from where you come from to where you may end up? I hate to turn sugar into shit, but all this wasted hot air and spit, inevitably, will be the main reason you end up dead or in cuffs.

I see you walking around all high and mighty now with your chest out and chin up, but I still don't see why you act so proud. Silence speaks volumes, just as one blessing can calm you. The power of life and death lies within the tongue, so even things you whisper, negatively, will somehow be magnified and loud.

I told him, I know exactly how it feels to feel alone and lonely in the midst of a crowded cemetery of animated bones of cronies. Then, he cursed me out, becoming exactly what he had shown me and told me, those people you speak of are family; more than just homies.

So, I then backed back further than I thought he could have thrown me and said, look, I think it's just the child or howl in me that loves to see a fellow wolf lead the pack. But, by judging the way you act, it's as if you want the meal, but lack the heart to kill. You just want it brought to you sealed, and packed in plastic wrap.

He quickly closed that gap, as if to attack, but only raised his hand to scratch his head and said that he didn't' understand. I asked him, why is it that robbing or shooting is in the common plan to get the things you want instead of working your ass off like the common man?

That's how you get people to respect the gangster that's within you. That's how you get what you deserve and earn by showing how the hustle still lives and will continue.

Only the wrong people will pretend to befriend you for your sinful ways of chasing your wildest dreams. When I was a child, I spoke and thought and reasoned as a child. But when I grew up, I put away childish things.

He shot back, things are not as they always seem, so you have to peep the scene. I get it how I live. Just like love and money in this land of milk and honey, sometimes I have to take it how I give.

He said, Ol' Skool, I just need everyone to chill and for someone to understand my pain. I know I'm not perfect and that my life may be worthless, but does that mean I shouldn't be allowed to play any position in the game?

I shook my head at his shame and told him that there was no time like the present to learn a new lesson and turn over a new leaf. And that the memories of the streets shouldn't be the only thoughts that he should be able to envision and see or have permission to keep.

I could now tell his thoughts ran deep as his mind peaked and he realized that he was the only wolf, in his crew, among a lot of sheep. I told him, there was once a time I didn't even cry for me or even try for me, while thinking logically as growing pains would follow me, yet I still hoped the Lord would see my soul as pure as olive leaves.

Then, he told me to accept his apologies for anything he may have said. We became friends at that moment before that statement was read, because I knew it originated from his heart before it reached his head.

Conversation Kills IX
Homeless Man

      He said I am this fucking city. And rain, sleet, storm, snow, or hail, even if things are pale or pretty, I will probably be here. You don't know my story, so don't act like you care, fear, or worry about my life on any night when you disappear.
      Ol' Skool, I need you to see my vision in HD, my position is like the world hates me, so let's just be clear, it was never my mission to be a plague on society. I don't require notoriety, and though I may sometimes stink like old rugs, I don't drink or use drugs, and I can pass any tests of sobriety.
      I've just been hit by a vast variety of bullshit that would make the average man a savage man and feel like a clueless guide on a useless ride to drive to commit suicide. And you and I both know that in this cruel or prideful world of do or die that even the innocent is soon to fry.
      I'm not used to pride holding me back from doing whatever I have to do out here in these streets to survive and make it. He said, as long as I'm here, alive to take it, I'm going to get it how I live as long as someone will help out and give, even if my uneven stride is naked.
      Ol' Skool let me try to break it down for you. How will you know where I'm at if you haven't been where I been or seen what I've seen; understand where I'm coming from? I then told him, there's no way I can walk a mile in your shoes, or a common run, and I know you have paid your dues, but so have I, and have had to live with those choices, even the dumbest one.
      Just like you, I am a mother's son who was handed these cards of life to play on my own. Only God can judge you, so I can't begrudge you because there are thrown parts of my life that I'm sure are homeless and haven't grown.
      He then said, but I'm sure society has shown you less hate and more favor. I've been cursed out, laughed at, and picked and spit on so many times that I can now taste the flavor.
      I've prayed countless nights to my great Lord and savior, but even His behavior has me questioning His existence. We live in a world of universal resistance where the innocent fry, the guilty prosper the wildest, kids act grown and adults are childish with no persistence.
      I've seen it all in an instance, so don't piss on me and tell me it's rain. This very moment is how far back I went, not how far I've came. I'm not asking to get out the stain, just help dealing with the pain.

My main mission is just to maintain a daily basis. Every day I have to deal with the tasteless that treat me like the fearful faithless whose blessings are unworthy of God's cheerful greatness.

He said believe it or not, on some cases, I've helped out others just from the goodness of my heart. Life's lessons have taught me to continue to try to be a blessing from the start, so the little gifts I do receive will never depart.

I blame no-one for the events that led me down this path. And even though I can't add up the math, I know there are some that are worse off than me, as you know and see, that not only have gone several days without a bath, but have also had to deal with the Lord's and the devil's wrath.

I still try to enjoy life all the while and laugh with a crooked smile, not to hide how I sometimes feel inside but to rejoice with each "nutritious" meal tried that was provided somehow with God's good grace. I could be mad. I could be sad. I've had mace sprayed in my face, been thrown in jail just for finding refuge in a resting place, and even after pleading my case I was left with no trace of justice or peace to increase my faith, but the bass of the His words in a deep space in my heart kept me at a righteous and steadfast pace.

I told him I know it's hard, seeming like every day you can't afford to let down your guard. But I'll ask you on this day to allow me to help heal the scars and rearrange those cards that you've been dealt to increase all life's wealth, so you won't be left living up and down the yards on the boulevard.

I told him I can't promise fast money and cars, just an opportunity to get to a better life. I thanked him for changing my tire in the rain that night because I was physically unable to get it right.

He gave me more insight of being a better man, no matter the circumstance, that made me realize how we as a people can neglect man. I now have a better understanding of the true meaning of life and God's plan. I now try to also be a blessing and help out all that I can.

Conversation Kills X
Lucifer

You can never bullshit a bullshitter. Ol' Skool, I know the Bible better than any man and have made many men lie, cheat, steal, or be a quitter.

You want to get rid of me, but the sins you've committed, I created them. The lies you've told. Shit, I created those too. Anything wicked, deceitful, or just down right wrong is me. I lie so much my truth is bullshit. He said, Ol' Skool, and I'm proud to tell you that there is no truth in me to get.

But there is one thing you got to love about me, I know the Bible; word for word, page for page, chapter for motherfucking chapter. Then I stopped him in his tracks and told him, that means nothing because the Lord is the one you've always deceived and been after.

And love and laughter has always defeated your hate. He then shot back, yet your people still kill and rape.

And I told him, yet we still keep the faith because the hell you come from wasn't made until the Lord made your ignorant ass. It's for you and all those who follow you because He is the one that decides when anyone's time has come to pass.

Before you became the disfigured man you see in the mirror now, He already knew if you'd have a reflection or not. And the ungrateful ones that you speak of that take after you, so with you in hell they will remain in a drought for eternity unliving without a doubt.

For God will not punish the uglies with the handsomes. He will gather his sheep from the wolves in your woods and shelter them in His own home where we will have many mansions.

Lucifer then said, well that's some random shit to say. But since you want truth, I'll give you the truth. Jesus was hanging from a cross with pins in his wrist, smelling like old vinegar and piss over you negligent fools. He preached the same truths you trying to preach to me, Ol' Skool, but you preaching to the choir; I'm not the one that needs to be in Sunday school.

So, you're just another one of those fools wasting your time if you're trying to stop me. No man can block me.

Sitting here running around Earth like God and Jesus are your friends. He say, well tell me this, Ol' Skool…why are you all getting more out of what they put in?

Jesus was crucified for your sins, yet your people parade around without acknowledging that. Then I told him, that's true. But, you were the reason for all of that. You were the reason he was stoned and stabbed in the back.

God never abandoned His son Jesus. He freed him from a tormented world for our sake. Then Lucifer looked me dead in my eyes and said, and your people still seem to never give back. They just take.

Your possessed flesh is bound to die in a suicidal mess. And that's when they'll be able to test my wrath and deal with the stress from my chest.

Then the next thing I asked him was what he was really doing here, since he *had* all the power. He said, I came to kill, steal, and destroy. I'm seeking whom I may devour.

He said I came to give you the same offer I gave Jesus many lifetimes ago. If you bow down and serve me, I'll give you all the kingdoms and palaces that I can show.

I shot back quick and said, I don't care if you can turn stone into bread and I was starving. I would never bow down to you. How can you give me something you don't even own? You lie so much, your truth is bullshit and history is the proof.

He then smiled and glanced at me in a deceiving way. And from the look in his eyes, I believe he knew that he wasn't going to persuade me on any day.

And like a phantom in the darkness he disappeared in the shadows. Saying that persistence overcomes any resistance, so I will get you as long as the wind blows.

Black Rage

I'm tired of writing. And to be honest with you, I'm tired of reciting. It seems like every time I turn on the news day and night I hear the same sad, worn blues of torn black people taking all these cheap hits. Police departments act like it's a time to kill, so now I'm on some real life free Carl Lee shit.

Something like an unchained, off-the-leash pit, you might as well scribble my name on the top of the back page of that all-time mad dog beast list as I convey the spark that made this "nigga, this spook, this combat spade" display his instinctive primal black rage.

I am that Black Plague, psychologically born, bred, and bought, building this country till my back gave, to struggle and die sad, crazed in this cracked maze of a bat cave as two-thirds of a person…the way your constitution counted this black slave.

So let's fast forward from that last trade of sad days to what's been happening in the streets of black life on a few of these past nights. Now, it's still more than enough to too much when you look, bet not whistle and don't touch. Hands up, but don't shoot. Truth is, like that ungodly scene of Rodney King, I'd rather take the stomping of boots than to pay that last price by getting shot in the back twice by some racially-corrupt beat-walking badged mice.

You will never get me to act right. What happened to serve and protect? Every person on this earth you inspect is not a worthless suspect that you curse and reject. We're all the same that deserves the respect you try to infer and collect with your force and fear of hurt and neglect.

But, no. You now have the racial nerve to select blacks for crime like words you connect with rhymes to curve and infect the minds of black people as you deviously profile. What went from a jealous stare from the way we carry ourselves to the strength in our naturally nappy black hair is now an envious low smile.

It has to stop. How did it get so wild? Now an 18 year old child is dead for no reason without a weapon in sight. Truthfully, this could be me the next time I'm doing me, fluently, into the night. So I might as well act like Huey P. and take arms to keep calm and proactively fight for my rights before they start treating me with cruelty or worse by shooting me or taking another innocent black man's life.

Let's get this right, there is now a war on American soil. And, if need be, I will lead the black infantry with infamy, in the sea, instantly, if I have to fight the bigotry. I'd ask for help, but the government seems to be distinctively occupied at the moment with giving juices and berries to royals or which country carries the oil.

Their values are spoiled. Routine traffic stops on the side of neighborhoods are homicide. Even before the dawn can arise, children are traumatized, left crying on mamma's thighs. And a black nation is just left to wonder why the longest rides can turn to a sad song of cries from the strongest eyes because it seems like routine stops are the warning signs for when it's time that the calm inside dons disguise and the youngest dies.

It's time to arm the wise with a common pride of black rage, personified. And I don't want to hear about how blacks kill each other all the time, when over the past few years, 83 percent of white folks that was murdered was by white folks' design. So, if you're not talking about white-on-white crime, don't try to trick me into putting black-on-black crime into this rhyme at any time.

Why do we get pulled over for tail lights just for you to provoke jail fights, but you act blind like those three pale mice when you see us broke down on failed nights on the side of the road? Look, every man with gold isn't for the falls and every man with dreads isn't for the cause, but that's not up to you to handcuff with a biased ethics code that contains a bullshit corrupted clause that even a clansman tries to hide under his hooded robe.

No justice. No peace. It's a large piece of just us dying in these streets. And now, even when we may need you, we know there's no use for crying for police.

And as a result, we are left dying and deceased for trying to release this internal black rage. Even if I die in their black cage, just remember that we are now living in the history books so you may as well keep the encyclopedia out. The revolution no longer has to be televised. We have social media now.

Dispel the Myth

I was honorably called by a strong black woman to be powered with this black fist and to come here and dispel this black myth. To defend the good black men that some black women tend to place bold in black print that we are black dogs with lifelong fleas or STD's that they tend to end up and lay with.

So I need you to allow this black man to just say and display this. I'm damn near pissed to the fact that I just hate this, that some of my own black female bloodline can place a black race of black men in a black box of sin as if we are all kin and possess the same black state of mind with no black face. Yet, can turn their noses up with disgrace at any white woman that was black enough to be submissive enough to put themselves in a black position for the tough black chase.

We don't all lie, cheat and steal or kill another black man's fate at will for our own selfish gains. We're not all crabs in a bucket saying fuck it, on the prowl for the next woman to suck it perpetuating these childish games.

I am the role model, the soaking wet with sweat, true-blue collar hard worker that's too hard to follow.

The black-suit charging, white-cop dodging, white-collar hustling professional black exec. I am the influential potential, the real man raising real women with respect, and if need be...I can be your sagging and doo-ragging rough neck that still brings home a tough check.

I am a bonafied black powerful man with a voice of inferno that can spin dirt into glass or reverse it back to black sand.

Raised strictly by strong black women from the beginning, yet my sinning is stereotyped from the mischievous grinning of other black women's personal past. And you wonder why your relationship won't last. Confrontation can preserve it fast, but if you got your home girl in your ear saying he deserves it last and he should kiss your black ass, the two of you are bound to clash and it's bound to fall to ash.

But, I'm here to dispel this black man's myth. Not that we may possess the biggest sex stick but the thoughts that we all tend to blame others for our hardships.

Yes...some may be lazy. Yes...some may even be blind, crippled, ugly, selfish, uneducated, broke with a low self esteem and crazy. But even if you find the right man, that doesn't mean he's the right man for you and he may not even want you because you may come off crazy and lazy.

So, don't get it twisted and hazy, we're not all intimidated by the success of a strong black woman. Just know you're still the woman and still have to stay in a woman's place and not throw it up in a man's face every time you see that opportunity is comin'.

Black women lets uplift the spirits our fellow black men. Don't see it as we're using you or pretending to be something we're not for the sake of your dividends...see it as an opportunity to inspire your black friend and expand his reasoning and knowledge to see life in a different light and comprehend.

We have to break down these separating barriers and not live life in the past day. If when you met him and he smoked cigarettes and y'all didn't clash that way...don't talk about the surgeon general and cancer down the line in no way. This is the man you fell in love with just buy him a sparkling new ashtray.

Worry about what you want to have and last today in hopes that you won't end up broken-hearted. The two of you knew what you were getting into before the relationship got started. So, if there was a child from that, realize that all black men won't leave that because they may be bothered. There are some of us that will still own up to our responsibilities and take care of a seed that was planted to be fathered.

So, black women...I ask of you not to let the merit of all black men be slaughtered by the actions of a few. I am not a crack dealer. I'm a strong black figure for you.

A father...not a baby daddy or the missing sperm donor. A nine-to-five worker...A heavy thinker and not a heavy drinker with no business hanging on the corner.

Not a woman beater. I'm a God-fearing believer. The head and not the tail. A black man that can love a black woman and not be another thug in jail.

So, hear and support me as I speak and yell and help me dispel these black myths. Let us become individual black gifts of one black unit and be powered by the strength and symbolism of this black fist.

Don't March for Me

If what happened in Ferguson, Missouri. is what I have to look forward to not see, don't you ever in your life march for me. If I'm ever murdered or executed in cold blood like some old thug by the laws, just stop and pause before you ever decide to ball your fists and clench your jaws; you should really just depart and flee, because I'd rather you just shut up and be silent instead of cut up and riot, so just go ahead light up a torch for me.

I need you to be smart and think of a solution from why I died. I need my revolution to be televised. The epitaph on my headstone when I'm dead gone shouldn't be polluted with cries, instead it should read, here, in the heat of a confusion of lies, lay a victim of an execution in disguise.

So, don't you ever march for me! Leave my heart on the streets, you can keep that optical illusion of guys and women chanting my name in vain with the inclusion of signs while sinning and you vandalize, tearing up the city streets, pretending to have a hand in hand for peace. Am I next? No, I definitely don't plan to be, but I know that I am already covered by the blood of the lamb of He, and there is still more work in this sand for me, even though I know this has never been the land of free.

There is no understanding key, the stars and stripes have been washed down and wiped with the blood, sweat, and tears of the guilty until proven otherwise. You have the police, the elite, and then those stretched out in the streets on heated concrete; those poor other guys.

I don't need tears pouring from my poor mother's eyes as she watches in shame of a people acting like fools, tearing up my neighborhood. I need you to embrace my mother, face-to-face my mother, then put yourself in the place of my mother and since she may live next door, make sure that your neighbor's good.

Honor me the way you should without everyone hearing through the grapevine that you may have been attacked by police K-9's and that they may have even used fire hoses or sprayed lines of people with tear gas because you were engaged blindly into ignorant hate crimes.

I'd rather have my grave primed with the love and support of my own people. This is not about the lesser of two known evils. Birds of a feather have always flocked together, but remember, that I have always been an earth-toned eagle.

So, don't you ever march for me. If I die, don't hold a grudge, just know that my judge sits high and looks low. Vengeance is mine, says the lord. Yes I want you to take action, but don't get on one accord and die by the vicious blade of that same sword.

Allow me to be that ignored aroma of black flesh rotting on blood-stained gravel. The dust disturbed from a soul-piercing gavel.

I know I am the fuel that traveled to your anger. But, don't get into a duel with danger. Go after the trigger finger. Don't hurt the stranger.

Let me become the crooked bullet and the wicked ignorance in a fleshy container that pulled it that unraveled your hearts to grow cold and harden. I bleed the same crimson, thick blood from Emmitt Till to Mike Brown, and Eric Garner, then back around to Jordan Davis and Trayvon Martin.

I'm the bone-chilling sound of poison from the prison warden that a guilty man will never see. I'm even the rope burn left after a lynching of an innocent man on the bark of an oak tree.

And hopefully, one day I'd live to be the soaked feet of elderly, just bruised and blistered from the abuse of mister, still living to tell this story. I'm the voice of ghetto youths' worry in unfamiliar territory.

The pride before the shame. The eyes before the slain. Yet I cannot complain because I'm still here to address the lies before the pain.

So don't you ever in life march for me If I'm ever murdered or executed in cold blood like some old thug by the laws, just stop and pause before you ever decide to ball your fists and clench your jaws.

Fight for the cause and to be smart soon and go after the man that scratched his itchy trigger. Win my battle in the courtroom to execute the man that thought it was okay to shoot this "lil' nigga."

But, if that don't work, and there's no justice in the picture, and you've done all you can do, peacefully, around town, just be safe out because I support you as and want y'all burn Hollywood and Wall Street to the ground.

Educate Yourself

From the cheating father, to the monogamous mother, the highly-praised church sister or homeless brother; the gay lover and even the purse-snatching mugger and drug smuggler can be an involuntary host of HIV. Any straight man/woman or any gay I see. Even someone in the line at a buffet I meet.

High class, low class, in class, no class…must I take out time to remind you. Look to your left, look to your right…it can even be the person behind you.

From the no-collar crackhead to the blue-collar hard worker, instead, or maybe the white-collar exec. Not even the politicians and lawyers can't tell enough true lies and escape from the consequences of unprotected sex. It can even be you…and you just might not even know it yet.

Anyone can be next, so educate yourselves and get a test to know your status. It's better to find out and know from your doctor than any person you may have had sex with that may have this.

I'm not trying to make it harder by saying you have to stop having sex, but if you have multiple partners in bed, use protection so you won't feel at your saddest. Even if I found out that way, I then would be at my maddest.

So use some type of sexual apparatus because it's mainly transmitted though bodily fluids when you start to do it. Your life should be more important than to let a few moments of orgasm conclude it. This can completely change your life after you pursue it and go through it

So, don't you misconstrue it, no…you can't get HIV from a sweet kiss on the cheek. But, yes you can still get it from any oral sex underneath the sheets.

And no…not even when you greet someone with a hand shake or from sitting on a toilet seat. Not from touching a door knob, a water fountain, or any hug of brotherly love you might see would have you scorned. This is not a virus that's food or airborne. It does not live outside the body, so any casual contact will not have you in a position to mourn.

Educate yourself. Don't rely on anyone's appearance of health. And if you're unsure about anything else, there are many centers to go to that you can ask for help.

You never know when you're in danger. Yes, you can even get it by sharing needles with friends, and no…you don't have to worry about a stray cough from a stranger.

That can be an internal anger that you carry around for the rest of your life. Something that could have been prevented on any night, only if you would've taken the time to find out a way to educate yourself and do it right.

H.I.V. is an S.T.D. that causes the A.I.D. virus. There is no cure. Not now for sure. From the lowest on the social chain to the highest. From the richest to the poor. There is no minus.

There shouldn't be the slightest idea in your head into taking that chance. On the other hand, if you already have it and know it, you should let that other sister or brother know it in advance before you start courting for romance.

So step up your intellectual. Think before anything sexual. Don't let your personal enjoyment be your downfall. And, remember…the only 100% way to prevent it is to abstain and not have sex at all.

Faith without Works

She told me that having faith is believing in God. And that trust is like having faith in man. That is the exact set of words that she said. But I need you to believe and trust me when I say it that a faith without any works is absolutely dead.

You just can't be scared to spread your action towards your faith. You have to speak your better life into existence. And since persistence overcomes any resistance, just a daily behavior in thoughts of our Lord, a savior in good faith will forever penetrate the devil's defenses.

I mean, at any instance, a compromise with sin can become an ultimate surrender. Which means if you allow yourself to be controlled by a sinful hold, you make it hard for the Lord to be your defender.

God should be the only contender because He and his omniscient presence will never be a pretender in your spirit. Even if you walk through the valley of the shadow of death and evil, and you're near it, His hands, being divine will guide you along that righteous line so you will never have to fear it.

Because in your soul, His voice is in control, you should hear it…that unmistakable gospel that can calm any hostile-like water over raging fires. Remember, patience is a virtue and if it's meant for you, time never expires. Psalms 37 verse 4 states that if you delight yourself in the Lord, then he shall give you all of your hearts' desires.

All that you admire…this is just one of God's many promises given for a righteous life. You just have to discontinue with the bullshit and negative people in your life to completely live free without the strife.

Stop giving in to a lust for one night just for a sweet sensation in your groin. Man should recognize and love the woman that completes the other side and soul of him at heart because woman is cut from the rib of man's tenderloin.

You will then be conjoined by the power and blessings from God's grace. A couple that prays together, stays together. You have to vocalize your faith to assure your rank in that divine race.

Jesus had to first rise from his place before he called out to the storming rains, "peace be still." And though his followers seemed to lose their faith, he still delivered and proved that the power and strength of his word was real.

So tell Him and express something you can feel and allow your soul and spirit to unwind. You know what they say, He might not come when you call, but He's always on time.

And I want you to remember this line because it doesn't matter your faith, whether your messenger is Jesus, the honorable Elijah Mohammad or Buddha. That doesn't matter as long as you act out on that faith and received the message when it was coming to ya.

Forgiveness

Dear God. Forgive me my lord for I have sinned. As I stand here before you at your merciful hands I admit that at times in my life the demon's semen has leaked in me and corrupted my soul from within.

Pretending to be my friend while trying to control and console my entire spirit. Walking my thoughts down the valley of the shadows of death, yet, I did not fear it and was able to sanctify myself with terms of endearment in your mercy and glorify your name. Allowing Jesus Christ to attain my soul and gain access to my heart and obtain my spirit to override all evil thoughts committed polluting my brain.

So now I stand before you at the pearly gates truly repenting my sins and turning my life over to you, my Lord. I rebuke Satan's ill-willed rewards and refuse to die living my life between a war of the worlds behind the cruelty of his double-bladed sword.

So I beg of you to record the fact that I seek your antidote and graciousness for everlasting life. Through this fast session, this is my last confession that I've learned life's lessons from trials and tribulations and have devoted my time on earth to be a life without strife.

By accepting Jesus Christ as my Lord and savior. Becoming my salvation. Freeing my tormented soul from the devil's hold at the crossroads and leading it down a path of righteousness away from eternal damnation.

So give me your blessings and evaluations as I confess all of my convictions. Your son sent from above died from a cross crucifixion and rose though your grace from his tomb three days later disregarding any and all superstitions.

I want to purify myself and be ridden of any sinister thoughts and deeds. By rectifying my soul and trusting in my faith to show you in my heart I truly do believe.

I am only a disciple of your ancestry trying to relieve my dedication by trying to live a life that's completely free from me drowning myself in my own sins. The enemy of my enemy is believed to be my friend so Lord please let me pass and come in to your sanctuary and end this prayer and praise with a simple Amen.

Ghetto Evolution

At the end of this stand, I want you to stand, snap or clap your hands to let me know if you can understand this command and demand that I ran to land in your hand and you're paying attention and truly understand what I am saying.

You see I'm a young educated and very agitated African-American man just riddled with the complexities, injustices and irrelevancies of an ironic white-owned black society with inconspicuous dimensions of gimmicks that seems to be out for my people and me.

Delegating, relating, and contemplating about the old heads that used to stand on the corner preaching a good word, yet manufacturing and distributing contraband and herb off the curb contradicting themselves and their own words evolving into their own hypocrisy in the fallacy of a hazy reality dying from the blade of their own sword.

Some even wonder if there was a conspiracy about the absentee democracy involving the African-American minorities' vote and polls from the latest US presidency. Sad to see and say the absence of my people that day wasn't the scapegoat "white man" or any conspires of a well-thought out conspiracy planned towards me.

You see, I've come to see and realize the priorities, values, and morals of your average black man are twisted in the sense that the actions and thoughts of another sista, brother, or lover dictate our actions toward any other. Competition from brother to brother or the jealousy of another lover undercover has intrigued me to uncover my own philosophical, psychological views of others which may be difficult to understand or for another brother to even discover.

Even further, it's the implied duty of a mother to smother the black child with the technology of common knowledge and engrave into the mind of mankind to take his time, say what's on his mind, yet be sublime at the same time and that time is of the essence in his existence. The presence, persistence and pursuance of benevolence, intelligence, common sense and street awareness is essential to a black child in adolescence with much consistence and no tolerance for negligence or there could be a dire consequence more intolerable than ignorance, insolence, or incompetence.

Let us influence him to become omniscient to the science of relevance and about how the wealthy get richer and the poor and helpless stay the same. Who's to blame in this game of pain, fame, and shame? I guarantee most, if not all, niggas will point the finger or speak of the white man's name in vain to blame.

You can't complain, it's too clear and plain to see what a black man acquires and obtains as he reels in a little power and cash. It's cold as rain to maintain that flash of buying fast cars, big rims, or hundred-dollar jerseys of players from the past just to cover your own ignorant, naked black ass.

Most, if not all, niggas pass that test and are still blind to the success of the issuance of stocks and bonds or any economical chain of command. Just understand that the so-called white man should not be the only man that demands that master plan of political views and concepts and the basic principles of supply and demand.

What black man, better yet Afro-American, will stand to make a considerable contribution of distinguishing the aspects of an inevitable, yet suitable solution? The distribution of knowledge is the only reasonable resolution to the pollution of this illusion with no persecution of a white-owned black society with confusion in its predominant conclusion dying from its own merciful execution.

There's no real confusion in this delusion, just the countless temptations and procrastination of a black nation trying to prolong the racing sensations of admiration and celebration with no gravitation pulling the destination of a nigga against his own creation.

The only explanations of this complication is the exaggeration of flash and front, or sex, lies and videotape that the media sometimes seems to advocate. Some niggas will argue and say it's a piece of cake to create a black America without hate within but without white America and be self-contained without having even one mistake.

What does it really take to embed into the cerebral of black men that white men are not the enemy but are the competition in this world and game we are destined and forced to play. Any given day we dress to impress our own race even if faced with financial adversity, heartache, and stress and strain. Curiosity killed the cat but why can't we drink champagne and toast to impress all races with our success and dress to impress as we possess the best intellectual brains.

Let us begin to train the membrane of our future in the first initial critical, quizzical, metaphysical years of life so they will at least obtain a simple mental and beneficial clue to absolute fame when time is due. Through years of receiving and perceiving various views I've been inspired to pursue my own historic, metaphoric clues and am gladly open and willing to issue all my point of views out for reviews.

My inquiring mind has rendezvoused at a new conclusion to a ghetto evolution producing an African-American, from a nigga in the dark, with a new-found respect for select situations and subjects leaving me with some of my own opinions and thoughts to object or correct.

For example, and with all due respect, a child support check shouldn't be the direct retaliation of aggravation from one slick bitch to a slicker nigga, 'cause his dick creeped, had an enigma, and figured to dig deeper and sleep with a richer and slicker sista

Really, let's be serious, you should be bigger my sista, even though the nigga fiddled and triggered your emotions, vengeance is neither the question nor the answer. Don't get me wrong, revenge at first feels sweet, but now the thought enhancer of reconciliation is obsolete and can now eat away at you like the malignant cells of cancer.

So now, what's the answer? Better, yet, what's overall the question so I can discover my own answers through my sessions of progression of trial and error? I'd rather experience my own terror so I can be more clever and appreciate more the figure looking back the next time I stand tall and upright facing myself, staring into the eyes of the reflection in the mirror.

Make my vision clearer so I won't despise and hate a white man today for my people's cries and fate back in the days of white man's take in the days of slavery. That pain is somewhat a beneficiary and necessary in a sense that we extend our vocabularies, grow stronger, and acknowledge our black visionaries and fewer worries on more occasions other than the few days in February.

Let's not be at all scary to rise up 'cause we don't have any reason for shame of that pain. We should just find a better solution. Cause I'm not trying give off the illusion of a conclusion, a ghetto revolution. I'm just making my justified ghetto contribution for the simplest solution for the fusion of an upgraded, disillusioned and revitalized ghetto evolution.

I Am Black Power

On this very day, I found out that I'm not invincible. Instead I've become invisible like latent heat, I'm no longer sensible with a divisible state of mind. And only on precise principles do I find that I am impenetrable like the Titanic.

Yet my thoughts will never sink or try to panic even though sometimes I just can't stand it when I am tested by the havoc of icy waters in turmoil. Even though I'm known to slick a can of oil and bullshit the bullshitter into crying over a glass of spilled milk that may be spoiled.

Some say the greatest trick the devil ever pulled was convincing the world he didn't exist. So, I'm going to tell you this. They call me Ol' Skool. A black fist with pride pissing on a white lie risking its fate to never hide or divide.

I'm a poster child for a suffering dried black nation with no poster. The most powerful voice ever heard with no vocal chords and a silenced tongue. I know for a fact that when you've had people tell you all your life you'd be a loser behind your back, it's kind of hard to realize when you've already won.

But, I am God's son. A born project nappy head prodigy promoted to the greatest ghetto spokesman. I am as soothing as an ice-cold coke can, but I can also be the leader of Al Bundy's club called, "No Ma'am".

Born with a natural smoke tan, I realized at an early age that money tends to rule all. But just remember when your outgo is more than your income, I guarantee your upkeep will soon be your downfall.

So, you have to always stand tall because your attitude determines your altitude in this world. Life can be a long journey stretched out on the wrong gurney on any night if you cross the wrong boy or girl.

So stay humble to yourself. And when faced with adversity, never be too proud to ask for a little help.

I mean, I once tried asking my right-hand man to hold me up like a belt, but forgot, I was on his left and realized my friends were close, but my enemies were nearer. Yet, before I could ever judge another man, I knew to first always examine the man in the mirror.

So I did that. Testing my reflection to make sure any corrections made were self-made and not influenced by another. Not influenced by sinning, but instead, as I watch the unworthy fall I feel I can build my dominion as a dedicated brother.

One of God's greatest gifts blessed with a shifted voice. Ignorance can be hereditary and bliss…but stupid is always a choice.

So rejoice in my gospel as my words began to trickle and shower. I am all over, yet, I can never be physically seen. I am black power.

If You Knew Better

To all my black women, it's said that if you knew better you'd do better. But, instead, of stepping your game up, you just blame stuff on other women because, even in black or blue weather, you know they could wear your high-heeled shoe better.

This is my new letter stating that no man wants to be in a relationship with drama and sex in a land full of hurt and commotion. And I promise when I say this, I'm just being honest to display this notion…all this good sex that you claim to have is just a great fist, stroking with a hand full of Aloe Vera lotion.

So contrary to popular belief, while you are going through all the better motions, remember, sex won't make him love you and a baby won't make a man stay. If you knew better, you would do better, so I'm making sure you know better to show better that if you let a fool kiss you, it's stupid, but letting some stupid kiss fool you is far worse on any day.

You shouldn't be a woman that needs a man. You should be a woman a man needs. But, instead of trying to meet a man, you just want a man to meet demands of magically taking care of your needs.

So, let me be the first to say, trick, please. Anyone can make you happy by doing something special, but only someone special can make you happy without doing anything at all. They say home is where the heart is, but if that heart is broken, stop and pause, then turn your cell phone off because you shouldn't let any random man make house calls.

But, that's just a lost cause. Even if I knew then what I know now, I'd be different, I'd change and would slow down. It doesn't take a lot of spare change to pay attention, that's why silent has the same letters as listen, but you take a man's silence as permission to go out on the town like a clown to paint the town red and brown.

So don't lower your head and frown. If you knew better, you would do better. Stop going around spending money you haven't earned to buy things you don't want, to impress people you don't even like. A man is only insecure about a woman when he knows another man can treat her better, but your insecurities are with other women taking your man for one night.

If you treat him right, you don't have to worry about a man leaving. And if you make love to him right, you don't have to worry about him cheating. But, if he doesn't work, he shouldn't be eating. He don't help, he shouldn't be sleeping. He don't try, he shouldn't be dreaming. He don't make love, he shouldn't be skeeting.

You shouldn't be bleeding while he is healing. You shouldn't be grieving while he's reeling in all the benefits of a burglary. Never trust a bald vegetarian in a wheel chair that doesn't eat animal crackers with dandruff in his hair and dirty shoes, and never try to put a band-aid on a wound that needs surgery.

I'm not trying to give you the third degree, but we live in a society that teaches women not to get raped, instead of teaching men not to rape women. Sex appeal is 50% of what you got and 50 % of what others think you got, so stop grinning, dressing, greasing yourself up and spinning like a piece of hot rotisserie gold chicken.

If you knew better, you would do better. Don't be afraid to make mistakes. Be afraid of not learning from the order of mistakes you make. You shouldn't hold on to nothing and still be afraid to let go. Go to church because if our steps are ordered by the Lord and His grace, how can someone else show you that you're out of order on any date, and how would they know?

When I put on Jordans, it doesn't help me play better, but when I put on the word of God it sure helps me pray better. Even if you take more hits than Floyd Mayweather, you're not going to be here forever, so don't just live and receive. You are only here to give then leave.

You see, in school, you learn the lessons before you take the test, but in life you take the test before you learn the lessons. If you hit rock bottom it's a good solid ground and a dead end street is a good place to turn around, so go out and get your blessings.

I mean, it's funny what some men will do and some women have even given their consent. Don't miss this message and think about it. Some single women are currently in monogamous relationships with married men and it seems like they are content.

How do you insist on finding the right one when you're still worried about where the wrong one rests? If you knew better you would do better, so never leave someone good in hopes to find better because once you've realized you had the best, Mr. Wrong may have found a better woman to undress.

Men don't treat you right just because you may wear tight clothes with all your stuff sticking out. Chivalry is not dead…ladies, it's just called tricking now.

So, instead, while you just look up at the roof of the church, glancing at the preacher telling the truth and it hurts, I just want you to stop acting like someone else. Auditions are currently being held for you to be yourself so go ahead and act out. If you knew better, you would do better, but I guess you didn't know what it's all about. So if you can't say amen, just say ouch.

Harsh Reality

I need you to listen at me and let me learn you something about this crass, harsh reality. Until you've truly tasted good pussy to the last starched calorie, you'll, forever, be satisfied with the asshole. And, it only seems greener on the other side of the fence because there's a man knelt down in bad clothes with a paint bucket and other fertilizing shit where the grass grows.

Smiling faces distort on lying sad souls because even mom and dad knows that unprotected feet is what helps those kids catch colds in these streets.

It's funny because you would rather me use a catcher's mitt to catch you from falling in love when you fall asleep than to catch you from when you creep and fall in the hands of temptation. So, it seems to me that you're more afraid of catching feelings that would have you fall on bended knees than catching a sexually transmitted disease or something worse that makes you fall that a doctor can't even catch with his medication.

How can we head this nation when you only love it women call you daddy during sex, but hate it when they call you and tell you that you are going to be a daddy from that sex. And this is just something that I once read and saw in a text that some women are only on birth control so their side nigga can take it, rape it, and naked next, but allow me to go ahead and digress.

I mean, some will mess with the next and the next unless he's the best every day, and let him hit raw, but then have the nerve to wear a shower cap every night like it's the law to protect their forever changing weave. You won't date a man that's living with his momma but will sleep with a man living with his wife, but, maybe that's only strange to me.

You can't believe everything you see. A sight for sore eyes can lack vision, so forget eye candy in your peripheral when it catches your attention. You need to be soul food, but remember it's some hungry and thirsty old fools out here that will talk about side chicks all day, so rude, but spend all night trying to convince a woman to let him slide through, while she lies nude, just to be that side dude.

You see, there are many ways to divide you, so let me enlighten you and lighten your load by supplying you with something that may be a little too heavy. No matter how great of a woman you are to a man, you will never be good enough if he is still not ready.

I'm not trying to be petty, but you should choose the man that taught you something rather than the man that bough you something or a cheap thrill. His desire to see you make it should be greater than his desire to see you naked because a good woman is a great investment. A bad bitch is just a steep bill.

You can't be out every Thursday, Friday, and Saturday evening looking for a babysitter with Tupperware to heat meals so you can spend the night at the club, then struggle to catch Sunday's service with love and back to the Sunday night alcohol and drugs like that life is a habit. Stop trying to be bad and boujee, because it's really just righteous and ratchet.

I mean if its right there, you grab it, because despite how open, peaceful, and loving you may attempt to be, people can only meet you as deeply as they've met themselves. And that may be what breaks you. Let me give you a great clue. If you didn't tell your friends so much of your secrets when they bait you, your enemies wouldn't know so much of your business to degrade you. It's some of your day ones that have been plotting and hating on you since day two.

So allow me to wake you, because I love to share and will never forsake you, even if it seems unfair. How can a single person say they're too busy for you, but say they care, when they're married folks with kids, careers, cooking, and car repairs that still find time to have affairs.

Even if it's one of your nightmares, just know that it's better to know the lie and learn the truth than it is to discover the truth after living a lie because false knowledge is far more dangerous than ignorance.

There is no winning this. Men lie, women lie. Women need to feel wanted and men want to feel needed. You would think this is common sense. But, since common sense has never been too common when you see it, it's just a common twist.

Your mental capacity shouldn't contain a malnourished glitch, like a convict is in solitary confinement when he's hungry for sex, stomach growling for free world chefs with a thirst for a presidential pardon. I have a seductive tongue with the mind of Darwin, because it was at that very moment that I truly tasted good pussy that I realized how much I had really been starving.

Inspiration

It's a known fact that in life you have to do things that you hate to do or don't want to do in order to get where you want to be. And as long as you know and understand where you come from, there is no limit to where you can go and what you can see.

The body can be tackled. Arms and legs may even be shackled. But the heart and soul of a man will never crackle as long as his mind is willing to scavenge on knowledge for truth like a black-backed jackal in the wild. In the depths of darkness and defeat I still can cool the heat with bruised and blistered feet and produce a swollen smile.

You're looking at God's golden child. He is my witness and Jesus is my poetic sensei. So listen to what we say, their words are spoken through me. This is Amistad, and I'm trying to give us us free like Cinque'. Breaking away from the usual suspects like Sosei.

Something like the eighth wonder of the world. Eight times a day I wonder what I can make up to say that's inspirational for the sake of young misguided and undecided, wondering boys and girls.

Making my poetic invasion. Infiltrating the minds to let them know you don't need a prerequisite to the curriculum just to be a part of the mathematic equation.

Multiplying the time needed to divide the added stress by subtracting the added mess so we can equate up to the highest power. And under God's grace and blessing will we and our people ever be restored and revitalized under His reigning shower.

So it's either get busy living or get busy dying. If you don't stand for something you'll fall for anything, so it's either, win the fight to live a better life or die trying.

As you can see, I'm on a higher tip. Ancient Egyptian hieroglyphs are carved in my head in mighty scripts and the melodies from the choir's lips are imbedded as their voices rise and dip.

Piercing my heart and soul like hollow tips as I fall to my knees and pray. In order for our children to be leaders of tomorrow we have to learn from yesterday's mistakes and become an inspiration for them today.

Because in no way does your past have to dictate your future in the present. So listen. Experience is the mother of wisdom, failure teaches success and having faith in a mustard seed can move mountains if you let it and stay pleasant.

Because we are only stray peasants in God's kingdom. Even if we praise dance, lift every voice and sing 'em, it means nothing if the faith is lost in the king's son when He brings him.

You have to believe him, receive him and accept him as your lord and savior. Actions speak louder than words. You can say and teach the word, but it means nothing, it's more about your behavior.

Stop sinning. Stop pretending. Brothers, we need to become men and stop bullshitting and cheating on our women.

Did you know there are more collect calls on Father's day than on any other day of the year? That just tells me that most fathers are not around and our children are left primarily for a mother's care.

The responsibility, we need to share. Men need to love their women and women, let's not be too quick to dog 'em. Let's find a better way to solve 'em. Because if I care more about your life than you do, we need to find a solution because that's the main problem.

Don't let a judge tear apart a love that was joined together before God. We must become role models for our children that love can stand the test of time against all odds.

Even though I've lived from piddle to post, I'm still realer than most because I have a vision. The merit of a man is no longer judged by his character, but what's on paper. So you have to live your life and make your decisions within that life with precision.

Don't worry about a hater talking down on your name, it's their job to hate someone and have someone to blame every night. And if you don't have at least one hater in your life on any given night, you just might not be doing your job right.

Give them something to hate about. But learn to disagree without being violently disagreeable by cussing them out. Better yet, become an inspiration for them and open a helping hand to help them out.

And if you ever feel down and out just remember that crying only makes your face wet and stress only makes you fret and sweat over time. As a people, we should never be with the water over our head and not drown because the concept missed our minds.

Look. Listen. Learn. And inspire. So we can become a people that our children are supposed to admire.

Lethal

Poisonous. There seems like there's no longer joy in us. Subliminal shots to the brain. Another influential brother slain for trying to maintain and remain focused on his own legal voyages.

And lethal is my injected syringe and needle to the cerebral of a people that's forced into a position fetal from the lesser of two ignorant evils…a grown fetus that needs us to be us and not an insignificant weasel and cheat what's worshipped under a holy steeple…God, almighty…the only source that's significant and regal.

I am the starving eagle salivating spit for lip balm, mentally strapped, equipped with an atomic bomb like a kamikaze Viet Cong from Vietnam and the detonator for any destined hater is not packed in my palm strapped to my thumb…it has been surgically implanted from the root of my wisdom tooth, mapped out to the tip of my tongue.

And I explode from within… dispersing knowledge like hot shrapnel that crackles deep within closet sin. Spinned from the same composite skin, we are not the opposite kin…but instead sisters and brothers from other mothers' lovers stuck between another rock and a hard space in time since time's clock first went from tick to tock and started to begin.

You see, in the beginning Cain killed Abel. It's in the bible, not stapled…a brother's rival…such a shame and not a fable. But now cocaine is a label sold to our own tribal stable. And we're to blame for repeating this cycle from the archival that's fatal…choking our own people with the complexion of sable just to seem stable for material survival, committing homicide to suicide with no revival strangling our own people with a barbed wire cable.

We are all able. My words scratch death and bleed life, without pitch black darkness surrounding a soul's breath from an animated carcass on any night, how could you appreciate light? This is one of the first moments in my life without strife or a knife, but it ain't even about me. Yet you feel you still got to watch me because you can't stop me.

Just to feel safe under the space behind superman's cape, they put us behind bars to have a fate in prisons…not knowing what's really unsafe is the educated thoughts that I'm spitting with precision charged from the faith that unravels and stands in my spiritual visions.

Scalpel in hand making a biblical incision. Gavel in hand, God never judges with a cynical decision. Yet, on gravel, we, as man will give each other an involuntary clinical admission.

Lost souls travel lands to crossroads to stand facing their own spirit. Lethal enough to fear it when near it, yet your past will remain written in stone…no need to blame a clone, you can never clear it.

So as one tear sits in eyes for you to visualize, see yourself inside a silent cage. Now materialize my violent rage with a voice that can terrorize your private ways.

What's more lethal? Poisoning someone else's mind…or having your own mind poisoned by the wrong people. Understand my message…there should no longer be a need for me to address it.

One Tear Ain't Crying

Through hell and high water, no life preserver, with gasoline drawers on, I'd starve a self-made slave into a grave to feed my daughter, castrate his master after, with laughter, if I have to complete the slaughter. Whatever it takes to keep the blood from leaking faster and keep the gauze on and for you to realize that I am my own martyr and that within me is an all-bone construction of God's throne.

This is reality. Harsh words more deadly than the fatality of sharp curves, all zoned for a broad's dome with big sticks and hauled stones. Man, I'd break all bones if my baby is crying. And I'd be lying if I didn't say that just about every day I pray that I never see a day when my child cries or gets carried away because of something I'm not doing…or should be doing. And I'm warning ya, just because there may be fluid boiling and drooling from the crack of my cornea doesn't make me any less of a warrior storming the front line to confront minds that may have conceptions of deception brewing.

No matter what *you're* viewing, my one tear ain't crying. My one fear ain't dying. Hell hath no fury like a white, racist, one man jury that sits and thinks that listening with alcohol in his drinks and one deceptive ear ain't lying.

No weapon formed up against me, even if it's ten feet, will prosper. No, that spear ain't flying within me because whatever *you* hear ain't trying to uplift or increase me, but instead shift and decrease me into something beneath me that tries to deceive me; wanting me to freely get lost in the wind like a leafy, friendly, yet sleazy enemy that's full of hot air when it's breezy, while haters sit there and grin. And once they realize that hating isn't working, they start telling lies to your friends.

You don't have to believe my demise ain't the end. I've lost jobs. Played against the odds. I've been robbed and chased by mobs. I watched my heart throb, cry, and sob, had someone tell me my baby's mouth should be swabbed, trusted the wrong broads to slob my knob, and been to a point where I felt like my child would starve because I couldn't even feed my own child corn on the cob. So, don't let this façade of what you think you may know about me maraud what the good Lord made of me into being unholy and fraud.

Being everything I am makes some people fear what they are not because it's easy to discard the obvious to guard yourself from everything hot and take cover. Yet, there's more bread and butter when you discover that there are other people that get hurt and use that as a lesson on how not to hurt one another. But then some make it worse by using that pain of being hurt to intentionally hurt other lovers or sometimes their own sisters and brothers.

A judgmental word is something you shouldn't utter because I'd smother the mother of a blind, crippled and crazy cyclops that has a stutter, choke him with my socks tied and cropped in five knots, take a fry pot and boil some eye drops, then drown him until the cry stops and his thighs flop or I'm shot by five locked and loaded half-cocked white cops in a high spot on the dry, hot sands south of Iraq when it's humid. "If you can't convince them, confuse them." "Carry the battle to them, don't let them bring it to you." The words of Harry S. Truman.

More than man or stupid human. I'm a son, a brother, a true friend and father with a huge grin, even when life or the idea ain't complying. I may not have anyone lying next to me every night, but it's better than having someone lying to me every night, meaning I'm loving my woman, my dear ain't trying, and even her friends in the atmosphere ain't spying.

Just know that this one tear ain't crying. My one fear ain't dying. And, this puppeteer ain't buying, so I don't need you to put your two cents in, I'd rather you pay attention with this penny for your thoughts than to sell your soul into being bought for a small buck because you never knew the heart of a deer ain't lion, or pissed enough to go fist to cuffs and miss the bus when it's enough to twist the trust of man's best friend into believing his own worst enemy has all flaws gone, while he sits and puffs, and grits and stuff, next to a clawed stone. My one tear can't cry you a river, even when everything is said and all gone. So, now it's time for you to suffer the memories, sweet and bitter, by going through your own hell and high water with your own gasoline drawers on.

Pissed Off Peddler

    I'm not here to be pretty. I'm not here asking for your pity. So, you can take that to your city. Take that sticky note to your saddity committee's throat, or any other man with low hopes and witty remarks about me smelling shitty with no soap or looking too gritty.

    Since you are without sin, go ahead and cast the first stone and hit me again at home, but remember you're not too pretty your got damn self. You don't have to come with me, you can leave me alone, I'm just asking for some got damn help. If Jesus is a shepherd of lost sheep, just ask me what life has cost me, and maybe I tell you how that damn sacrificial lost lamb felt.

    Armed with this got damn felt-tipped sharpie and no help, hardly with this 4x5 cardboard sign, I argue with myself one last time about what line to write in this small space to try to receive a stranger's monetary small grace and at the same time to enlighten the small state of man's mind about mankind.

    You see, if you never speak your mind, never mind what I speak. I'm just trying to let you know that the great of man's mind has never been too kind at all. Pussies are too quick to leak and beat the less fortunate like a hard dick, just because you act like an ass, just full of shit, when you can't find the ball.

    Well, let me remind you all that when it's your time to fall, even if you didn't commit a crime at all, you will cry and bawl when you see an ugly side of this world. Love becomes anger, friends become strangers, comfort becomes danger, and even helping hands become a strangler that can choke life like five elastic strands of fake plastic pearls.

    I can see it, now, in your eyes as your mind breaks in drastic twirls. I feel like I'm dodging thrown bricks. And you've just shown this, if there was time to help the homeless, we'd be the last chose. And I know that just as sure as I know that green is the color that money trees and grass grows. Society's past shows us our lives ain't worth shit, and if shit had any worth to it, poor people would be born on natural bare earth in unfertilized dirt with no assholes.

    All you see is a few sad souls, but we just fell on hard times. You should be lucky we haven't fallen on hard crimes.

    I mean it really doesn't make sense. You waste cents on relief efforts from every natural disaster to every impatient bastard with a gun in his basement with a mental factor, but have your face bent like a movie actor because I carry a flagrant fragrance from sleeping outdoors on the pavement.

You just need to face it. I, too, am worthy of God's greatness. Many times, for no reason at all, no matter the season you call, I've had to say this prayer with my hands behind my back in metal bracelets. So where is my placement in the Bible that you quote scriptures from with your face bent and pictures hung that you kneel and pray with? I thank the Lord daily, even though I feel like He won't save me with His blessings or any grace sent.

I'm not here to buy beer. I'm not here for drugs. I'm not here to cause fear. I'm not trying to be a thug. I'd like to support myself just as much as a diking, bull-dagging stud claims to be a woman so she can get in free for ladies night at the club.

But, I can only shrug and spend my time in pain from piddle to post, pissing in the rain, trying to eat from what I can peddle the most because I can't afford shame.

All I can give is a name. I have no callback number. Yes, I would love a job, but there's no address of where I live. So, I keep what I claim. I just walk in hunger. I would hate to rob, so I prefer access to what you give.

Is the reason that you've turned your back on me because I live out here on the streets, homeless, doing what I have to do to survive out here in this cold place, all alone? Or, maybe, the real reason is that I remind you of your lonely spirit and soul that roams around just as much in the cold and also doesn't have a place to call home.

So, I'm armed with this felt-tipped sharpie and no help, hardly with this 4x5 cardboard sign, arguing with myself one last time about what line to write in this small space to try to receive a stranger's monetary small grace and at the same time to enlighten the small state of man's mind about mankind.

So I'll just inscribe "what if you were I...and what would you write for me to help you out to get by," the next time you are on a mission. So, let's get this right, I was also made a reflection to be seen of God's image, but I would rather have an eye condition and go as blind as love at first sight than to be able to see, even through night and still find that I might be like you and have physical perception, but still lack vision to see the light.

Racial Injustice

I need you to listen to me my black brothers and sisters. Black society as we know it is dying and committing its own suicide. And it's a shame cause sometimes I wonder when I ride if I'll become the last victim of homicide or such dealings like the victims from the mass killings of the Rwanda Genocide.

Just trampled over by the iron feet of oppression. And I'll be the first black man to teach the last black lesson that black justice in itself is just another motherfucking black lie. Seeing that the blind and cunning black bitch has a stigmatism with high dollar signs for eyes.

Betraying the moral fiber with true lies like Benedict Arnold or a white wolf dressed in black sheep's clothing. Black history is not an accident. It's been the white choices of white ancestry since black times began when black males were bought or blackmailed and stolen.

Dividing and conquering my black kin like Napoleon insisting that my black pigmented skin has been a black sin. And some even infiltrated from within and portrayed themselves to be my next friend.

And we all fell for the okee doke. We were bamboozled, hoodwinked, or shall we say run a motherfucking muck. We've been the victims of violence way before Hiroshima and Nagasaki felt the first shrap metal from when Pearl Harbor was hit and struck.

And there still was no luck being that there were divided skies yet and still my black pilots were there to contribute. It's just too bad that racial exclusion continued on many years after the first black man graduated from the Tuskegee Institute.

So I ask myself. Why must all this racial animosity plague our black society? How can we remove this cancer without getting cut by the double-bladed sword of hypocrisy?

I'll tell you. First we must strive to create our own black America within but without white America without any outside help. It makes no sense to try and unite with other races if we can't even first unite with ourselves.

We must learn to starve ourselves and become hungry for knowledge. Educating ourselves, looking far beyond the mediocrity of a high school diploma but for excellence with a degree in college.

Let us recreate a solid 1921 Tulsa, Oklahoma black Wall Street before it was bombed by the KKK and other envious whites. That night's carnage left some 3,000 African Americans dead and over 600 businesses lost destroying a successful infrastructure in the fright.

Events that will forever be wrong and never made right. Which was something that challenged my faith and spiritual insight.

As black African Americans we've had to endure much racism, oppression, depression, and all types of social injustice from these ignorant white fools. There was an ill-willed talk of reparations for our ancestors' fate but I'm still waiting for the forty acres and they can keep the fucking mule. They can give me a lean to shack and a mad black poodle that drools.

Maybe we should combine the three theories of M.L.K, Malcolm X, and Huey Newton and have complete separation of the races in a non-violent manner and protect ourselves by any means necessary. But it's up to us to find what means are necessary and beneficiary and acknowledge those creative minds as true black visionaries.

And why is February, the smallest month of the calendar year given to African-Americans for black history. Because it's an all-out white conspiracy my black brothers and sisters.

If you take all the old US currency coins and truly look at them you would see what I'm talking about. The white slave owner presidents on the quarter, dime and nickel are made from silver and are facing to the left. And Abe Lincoln, the president that freed the slaves, is on the lowest cent, having the lowest value and is made of the brown material of copper facing to the right. As if he was opposing progression by looking back against the times. Some shit that caught my attention so there was no point in making it rhyme.

And this Caucasian persuasion had to be blind with the false accusations of my skin being a crime.
Creating Sambo cartoons and calling my people colored because we are black. Well let me tell you something about that. When I'm born and dead I'm black. Hot, cold, scared, sick, beat up and any of that I'm the same.

White folks, when you're born, you're pink, hot, you're red, cold, you're blue, and when sick, you're green, when you're scared, you're yellow and when you die, shit, you turn gray. You turn to just about all colors of the rainbow, so how in the fuck can you call me colored on any got damn day.

I'll be a rogue renegade before I respect any white man that has no respect for me. With all this controversy I'll never Uncle Tom up to anyone who won't let me be.

So now I ask you, what can we do about this disease of racial injustice plaguing our society like the early symptoms of a chronic epidemic? Well, I don't have such an answer for that, but we truly need to find the necessary means for a cure so we can get rid of it.

RIPTM

I'm the aroma of black flesh rotting on blood-stained gravel. The dust disturbed from a soul-piercing gavel.
I'm the crooked bullet and the wicked ignorance that pulled it that unravels a heart to grow cold and harden.
Everything from Emmet Till to Trayvon Martin.

I'm the bone-chilling sound of poison from the prison warden that a guilty man will never see. I'm even the rope burn left after a lynching of an innocent man on the bark of an oak tree.

And hopefully, one day I'd live to be the soaked feet of female elderly, just bruised and blistered from the abuse of mister, sitting on the dock of the bay to tell this story. The voice of ghetto youths' worry in unfamiliar territory.

The pride before the shame. The eyes before the slain. Yet I cannot complain because I'm still here to address the lies before the pain.

Self Made Man

Like father, like son is what the old folks in the neighborhood always told me. And the apple never falls too far from the tree, from what I see, is what they tried to bestow upon me.

But I'm nothing like my father. This was a man that always seemed to make my grandmother's daughter's life a little bit harder.

A man that never bothered to give a piss poor attempt to see and make sure his wife's son didn't step and fall in the footprints of a life that he was drug through. Instead, I mapped out the blueprints of my own life, although some were sinful, I struggled through the mud and dug though the bullshit to find what was true.

Through my eyes, his reflection was in disguise as I walked past any mirror. Just the fear of him and his bloodline, I was just in a flood trying to swim as he drowned in shame, but I also didn't want his pain to be any nearer.

The vision in my brain couldn't be any clearer from a man that was raised primarily by women. Learning everything I know, as the only boy on my own, you can see that I was headed for a life of mischievous grinning.

I was a hurricane, lost in the whirlwind, spinning. But, I blame him for absolutely nothing. I'm a grown ass man. I know right from wrong and can understand that I shouldn't fall for anything, but at least, stand for something.

It ain't no fronting, I've grown to be so strong I wouldn't leave me alone if I cheated on myself and ended up with bad health. I love myself unconditionally. And wouldn't give a fuck about anybody not feeling me.

I control the sin in me. It's not even a temptation to try to please y'all. If that was the case, I'd be like a crackhead in a race to sell what's left in my lost soul's place for the last speed ball.

I'm lost in my own addiction. Serving the sentence from my own false conviction.

Yet, I'm so confident and persistent; it tends to come off as nasty. I got the depiction of any true blue-collar hustler. I will bleed, sweat, and tear up for any dollars that pass me.

Some will even say it's blasphemy. But I'm a self made man, once pronounced a prince. I went to sleep and had a dream I went to bed with a queen. Then, woke up in that same dream and I ain't slept since.

So who must I convince? Flooded with a watered-down life of thin blood. I'm a self made man so I made myself into being a real man made from what man made push and shove.

Far from lust but I love a wet bush like a fitted glove, yet can't no man or bitch hug me enough to make me or break me. Even the trash has to be taken out so I volunteer to not pass up the chance to not let another man hate me.

And I don't give a good solitary fuck how it makes you feel. I have no point to sugar coat or brag and boast; I spit my life. I'm going to give you what I know is real.

And if anyone has the testicular fortitude to tell me different about the way I live. Feel free; I open up the platform. But if they're not a black leader, but just trying to lead blacks, I won't even take off my hat for 'em.

You get no respect if you're not self made. That's like telling a female you love them, steady lying your ass off just to get laid.

Or a female doing the same thing just to get the rent paid. Black women are the queen of the land and black men are natural-born warriors. And since integration of minds is just an illusion of inclusion, I try not to let bullshit concepts to travel past the peripheral of my cornea.

So I'm now warning ya. I got a graveyard disposition and a tombstone mind. I'm a grown ass self-made man. I don't ever blame my past for shit I do in the present time.

When I was a child I learned to decipher the rhyme between truth and bullshit like grad students. It was a long shot, but I was in a cage, trapped and enraged, I had to do this, I chose the righteous path instead of the righteous act for the sole purpose, because of my bad influence.

And for the others doing what you do to the fullest, I know it gets hard sometimes, whether you're a woman or a self-made man. That's why I do me to the best of my ability with only help from the praised man because that's the hand I was dealt and only way I can.

Sick and Tired

Now, I'm just going to be honest and get some random shit off of my mind. I'm so sick and tired of being sick and tired of people saying that you can't turn a hoe into a housewife every time that I see my female friends out nights trying to mingle. When the fact of the matter is, even with their spouse right at home, I've seen more housewives turn into hoes after the "I do" and wrinkled kiss of wedding bliss, more after they were the "good girls" doing hoe-ish shit when they were alone and single.

So, I plan to sprinkle and bring you the naked truth about some, not all, women. Yes, I'm talking to you. The one that will stop speaking your friends over the littlest things, but will keep grinning and forgiving the same no good, trifling, sorry dude, and making excuses for why he's so rude while he's fucking over you and sinning.

Yet, you're over here pretending to be the most authentic, the realist and the truest, but itching and bitching about fake men and women and how they will do this and that to unfulfill ya. They say real will recognize real, so why is it that you look so unfamiliar?

I'm here to drill ya...because I'm so sick and tired of being sick and tired of you going around saying that all men are dogs with an itch. Well, let me tell you something about that shit. Since you are what you eat. You are what you attract. So, if all you attract is dogs, maybe you're just a female wolf in sheep's clothing that bands will make dance, butt-naked to roll over and do splits. Just another dog ass bitch.

I mean, I get so sick and tired of being sick and tired of side chicks catching main chick emotions. If you're so sick and tired of starting over, stop quitting every relationship and stop just going through the motions.

A woman's heart and soul should be so lost with devotion in the Lord that a man has to go through Him and His gold to find it. So, how can you say you want a good man when you get on the internet, like Facebook, to post up close-up photos of you dressed up with your face hooked, showing your butt, sort of like perfume and lipstick on a bulldog/poodle mixed mutt and being surprised when a dog sniffs up behind it.

Let me rewind it. This is not for the simple minded. Even the devil can pose as baby Jesus, so hear me and believe this, when I say I'm so sick and tired of being sick and tired of you trying to hide it and keep what's right out of sight. Don't you know that everything that done in the dark don't need to come to the light? Maybe you haven't realized it yet, but everything that you have done has ignited a spark and glows in the dark at night.

I'm so sick and tired of being sick and tired of you not getting it right into your mind frame of change that a glass an hour will change an hourglass frame. The both of you can love each other unconditionally, but if your condition suddenly changes, he just may not show the love you the same and you may someday watch his ass walk out of a square piece of glass, surrounded by wood, and find out why they call it window pain.

I mean, true love will make you overlook everything in this game, except not getting true love in return. And, one of the cruelest things a person can do is awaken someone's love without the intention of truly loving them long-term.

A woman's loyalty should be earned and is often tested when her man has nothing. And, it really exhausts me to say that a man's loyalty is tested when he has everything like he's one of the best of the hustlers. But, since you're bragging about all the men that want you for something, just remember that the cheapest prices have always attracted the most customers.

I'm so sick and tired of being sick and tired of you being drowned in information just for ya, but you are still starved for knowledge as if it all has to be bought. The tongue has no bones, but is strong enough to break hearts, so understand when I tell you it isn't that ugly or unattractive men are designed to have more confidence. Maybe, just maybe, you're not as attractive and fine as you thought.

You have to stop allowing yourself to be caught up with the flash and front of swag and stunts of brothers flashin' money and saggin' funny like a gold digger with hood rat nerves. Find yourself a man with his pants on his waist that has more going for his case other than knowing how to hide and sack herbs because saggin' is really just niggas spelled backwards.

So, remember this, just because you may have some of the best black curves doesn't mean that you can get men to do whatever you want them to be willing to do. They may be just like me, and will get sick and tired of being sick and tired of dealing with you.

Step Your Game Up

I'm just going to cut out all the flashy talk on the mic tonight and just say some of the things that need to be said. Women...you need to stop bitching and moaning about a man you never really had, and brothers...you need to become men and step your game up before you lose your woman to another man that makes her glad.

Another man that makes her laugh because you refuse to do the things you used to do in the past. I believe any and every relationship can last...but some of us tend to be just too lazy to take the relationship out the trash.

For some reason, maybe you want to clash and be sad. Step your game up. Fellas...you need to change the same stuff you been doing because when you do what you've always done, you get what you already got. You can lose money chasing women, but can't lose women chasing money, so it's best to keep trying to build up your money pot.

And Sisters...stop comparing your man to someone else's man...because that is not the type of man you got and as much as you may want him to be in that spot, he will not, so just be happy with the good man you got and stop trying to change him into someone that he's is not...because SWAG, believe it or not, is just something we all got.

It just kills me how some women complain everyday till they have a headache in the brain about the man that they are with. Step your game up. If he is really all this pain stuff, why don't you just leave his ass and stop putting up with his shit.

And stop listening to the mess your no-man having home-girl may spit in your ear because she may fear your success and want you to be in the same position that she is. Anything that happens between you and your man is exactly the way I said it is...between you and your man and should stay at the place that you live.

Step your game up. Brothers...stop trying to blame stuff on others because you don't want to change enough and take charge of your life. You need to be the leader, the protector, the provider, and the believer in Christ because greater is He who is within you than any other man in this world on any night.

We need to live our life right. I know it's not always easy doing the right stuff...but it's also not right to always do the easy stuff. We need to step our game up...and find something that will change us into a people that will give us actions instead of useless thoughts when we've had enough.

For example, to keep it simple, be a man and take care of your kids…don't be a visitor that hits the door…become a parent and be a part of their life. Do what some of my friends did, even if your baby's mother isn't acting right, file child support on yourself and put them people in her life.

There's no need to fuss and fight or even be jealous on any night of another man speaking to your woman when y'all are out or at the club. There is no reason for push and shove…just be happy your woman is still fine enough and try using that other man's envy of you to strengthen you and your woman's love.

I need you to be far above and step your game up. And women…stop pretending; thinking you can change us into feeling sorry for a woman that won't even use her own common sense and education. Remember, there's no reason to try to control the wheel if you don't even know the destination.

We both need to stop our procrastination…because sometime a lesson told is better shown and the best lesson to learn is the one you thought you already knew. So if I told you that you should keep your faith, you shouldn't look at me in an awkward way like you have no clue and that doesn't apply to you.

You should try to do everything in your power to give praise to the highest power in your life. And I know I may be just a nobody…but I'm trying to tell everybody about somebody who can save anybody in just one night.

Only God can deliver justice right. The hardest fall isn't far, so fellas do what you can to be that good dude. And any enemies you may have, it's already been promised to you that they will be your footstool.

So as a people, let just keep our cool and be truthful because libel is lies written against you and slander is lies told about you. But rationalization is lies you tell yourself to replace the truth in hopes that others will see you in a different view.

Don't be busy trying to figure out what to do while others are busy doing what you're trying to figure out. Step your game up and shout if you hear me and know what I am talking about so we won't be thought of in the worst way. And if there is ever a moment where you feel like giving up on anything and cursing away, just remember why you held on for so long in the first place.

Sometimes we get so used to being broken that we don't look to be fixed... But just settle for not being broken anymore!!!

Strength Of A Black Woman

Can the strength of a black woman truly be measured in any way? Well, that's hard to say. There's really not any formula formulated out there to measure any lady or any real black woman of today.

For as long as I can remember and from what I've learned about in the past, black women have always had to hold, first and last, for lack of better words, the shitty end of the stick. Having to endure countless years of taking much shit from strict men restricting their lives with much bull shit so their future was not very hard to predict.

And that shit is so cold that most men in society still don't recognize and cherish the true essence of a lady to this time and date. Black women are sexually portrayed, beaten, betrayed or even raped before a first date has any chances of being great.

And now the weight of hate has maybe infiltrated and devastated the emotional state so much that the disgusting and degrading actions of one nigga can dictate a female's actions toward an other mate.

Not all females can relate to rape but most can relate to its consequences and repercussions of pregnancy and giving birth. No man can then challenge a woman's worth during the struggle of giving birth and not feel like a lurch the next time he sits in the back pew at church.

That shows strength of a woman. Not any man can honestly say that he would go through any labor nor have anything to do with a child for nine months in their stomach. And at the end, huff, puff, and push eight pounds three ounces out of a dime size hole because a fifty-cent piece size dick got aroused for a nickel's worth of time skeeted and leaked in it.

Or maybe need to have a slit cut under the navel because there may have been complications with the embryo inside it. Or even have the chances of a failed fetus because the sorry ass sperm donor caused problems because he didn't really want anything to do with it.

Even when a woman has a miscarriage an impenetrable and indestructible bond is broken between a mother and child. And all the while she may seem happy with laughter it's so obvious that there's a deep sadness hidden behind each and every smile.

Shit, and all the while, I tip my hat off to women just because they go through a menstrual cycle each and every month. Cramping, bloating, bleeding, mood swings, and not getting the sexual pleasure they want at a time when they have the most anxiety to release that intense sexual grunt.

And all these niggas do is want their females to please their sexual needs with lips, tongue and no tease to weaken their knees. All she should say is "Nigga please."

Then most leave and crawl under another she because he thinks his she isn't acting right. And maybe come back scratching and still won't admit his wrong doings but wants to fight.

Giving her a sexually transmitted disease. And nine times out of ten that nigga won't get checked in fear of her accusations of unfaithfulness of being right and his love life with her will freeze and seize.

So what strength of a woman is next? How about putting up with a nigga who uses love as an excuse or an alibi, or just a justification for sex? Most if not all past that test and still wants to rest his neck on another female's breasts or use them every two weeks to dip into their checks.

And some women have to put up with the wreck of arguing and fighting from baby daddies when the shit hits the fan and begins to fold. Being hit or even told from a future nigga on parole that's too cold and too bold to enroll his whole soul and become a diamond or gold and not the whole mold of a lump of coal that tries to control the whole household like a renegade Seminole.

The strength of a woman has no limits. Without being told some uphold the whole household, bring in the bank roll, disown that payroll, buy all the clothes, and condone and console his clone whenever he gets a cold. Dealing with a nigga that too sorry to stand on his own two feet and be a fucking man to see and support his own clone grow from young to old.

That's the strength of a woman. Loving any and all her children unconditionally. Never putting herself in a position to leave and never giving into temptation that would have her wishing to flee.

On their own some black women make time to work, take care of a sorry nigga's clone, relieve the pain of their own hurt, clean the home, and put up with life's jerks without even having fatigue on their face shown. That's the strength of a woman.

If I've said it one I've said it a thousand times. The strength of a woman has no boundaries and its limits are more infinite even more far beyond this simple rhyme.

Now let me put something more simple in between your temples and give it some light to shine. In these ironic times a woman has to deal with the stereotype of being called a hoe if she chooses to do some of the same shit a man may be acclaimed or proclaimed to being a real pimp, player, or ladies man of his time. Why can't a female play the field to find the man that will satisfy her and will wine and dine?

That's the main reason I cherish all women as the most priceless of treasures. Because the true strength of a black woman just cannot ever be measured.

Even a woman seen on the street looking her worst handling her business is the strength of a woman at its best. Therefore, the strength of a woman can not, has not, or will ever have a measure to test.

Hear Them Cry

From a seashell off the coast off of Africa 's shores I can hear them crying. The unrested souls and lost spirits of the slave driven from whip lash incision under white provisions. From photographic images in my mind I can truly see them dying. As the truth unfolds, you should fear it, not a figment of your imaginations or other hallucinations, but the frights on any night of the disturbed ghosts and tormented apparitions.

Without even asking for your permission let me take you out to the eye of the sea where the tears of the untold and unseen from fears have been wept and washed away unclean in vain and have truly been forgotten. I'm talking inconceivable scenes or epidemics of disease and being chained in between the knees of another even if that other was dead and rotten.

Before the picking of the cotton. I want you to seize the severe greeting to the nostrils from the nauseating stenches and from the inhumane fossils corrupting death's atmosphere. Can you envision the deafening shrieks of women and the groans of the dying exploding and trembling through your ear?

To be brought from a state of clear freedom and innocence, and, in a barbarous manner, be conveyed to a state of horror that can claim even the essence of a phantom's guilty conscience.

And influencing the violence in the dense fog, winds and rain were the thumbscrews and steel shackles, whips and chains or the cat-o-nine-tails. Which was nine cords dipped in tar with the ends retaining knots of pure hell and with no voice but when shot through the air could yell and tell commands by choice.

I want you to feel the claustrophobia fears override your mind in time from lying stacked spoon fashioned in spaces smaller than graves. And have your miseries from this brutal cruelty heard and carried out with each and every crash of the waves.

I want you to experience and capture a small taste of human waste of this hellish slave ship. Where there is no illusions of a myth; only floating spirits from the undead and suicidally-driven insane souls of the sick.

Now let me shove you back to the lower decks, women and children to the left, men to the right, and chain you by the neck with about 18 inches in between each deck. Congested with a plethora of future corpses, for lack of respect, that's crammed so tight there isn't room for even one single breathe.

So can you perceive it? Men strangling their brothers or women digging nails in the brains of other in hopes of delaying the suffer from suffocation. Victimized by the greed of the European nation and forced into comatose states from the small spaces where the air was never fit for respiration.

And having no sanitation so you are chained together on any night to a body that may be covered in lice and maggots and mice or blood from a fight or vomit from the urine and human waste from others that couldn't confine the sight.

A parasite that rapes and imbrues the character of all humanity. Molesting the rapture by means of fury and brutal capture that drives even the pastor to life's last friend, which is death or insanity.

And I am drowning in their tears. The violent tropical storms and hurricanes are the lost souls crying into the rains. With the lightning and thunder harboring their anger and releasing their agony from all their pains.

Creating this mirage of an oceanic abyss in a bottomless pit with crippled spirits that happens to lie beneath the seas of the middle passage of the Atlantic Ocean. This situation may be easier conceived than described yet being there to feel the emotion from this commotion is the only true potion.

No one here would second that notion to bear that motion of the uncharted waters. 600 overcrowded slaves rushing from the lower decks for fresh air, all bare-backed with no hat for starters, and, in the fury some even crushed their own sons and daughters.

No one was martyred but most were slaughtered for any and all that wasn't obedient. If you show sickness you're thrown overboard or rebel, you're hit with another cord, and choosing death over life was the most deviant.

The Atlantic Ocean is a sea of blood and misery polluted with grief and flooded with tears and agony settled on top of old slavery bone and ash. There's no wonder why I hear the cries through seashells or why the worst storms form over this ocean on any news station's weather cast.

So now I want you to listen very carefully to this last riddle and rhyme. Can you hear them crying? Close your eyes and allow your mind to take a trip back in time. Can you see them dying?

I want you to feel the shivering winds and freezing rains. Can you indeed feel it? I want you to relish the flavor and savor the scent of their blood and tears in vain from their pains. It's their lost spirits.

So tell me now can you hear it? There's no need to fear it. It's not us they're angry with on any night. Hear them cry. I want you to feel their pain or at least wonder if you would have learned about this shit in school if they were white.

The New

Same shit, different day. White America wipes their ass with blacks within every 28 days, making that period, the new cycle. Religion's the new weapon and cash, the new bible. It's like we worship the rifle. No longer the life you'll scope out and take aim. Guns, the new fist fight. Social media, the new brain.

Instagram, the new fame. Facebook, the new shackle and chain. I know a lot of men that love their kids to death, but child support's the new pain.

Teachers, the new parent. Internet, the new teacher. Baby momma, the new wife. Child molester, the new preacher. The shallowest of minds are the ones that feel deeper. Those with the most expensive tastes are the ones whose souls are cheaper.

Don't let them deceive you, candy paint with swangers on the slab is the new fever while whoever's child is acting out and being bad is the new leader. I bet I can make you a believer. Liposuction and tummy tucks, silicon injections and synthetic products is the new health. A full tank of premium gas and another man's trash, the new wealth.

A hard head makes a soft ass but correctional officer is the new belt. "Suck it up," the new help. "Acting a fool" the new "taking a stand." See a nigga, shoot a nigga. Cops, the new Klu Klux Klan. And a clinical needle at the hospital, the new trigger to the white supremacists' new population control plan.

Making fitting the description of another nigga or black man the new suicide. If the club is the new daycare, that means adults and grown folks we see are the new kids inside.

Turned up, the new high. Being real, the new fake. Waist trainers and all that damn makeup on the face, the new sexy. Netflix and chill, the new date.

Just like my homeboy Nate, I seen liars tell the truth and an honest man lie. Seen a weak man overcome and a strong man die. Seen a sinner render aid while the Christian stands by. Witness the guilty walk free and an innocent man fry. A calm man blow up. Sober man pour up. Dependable not show. And the undependable, show up. So, you know what, that's why the solution's the new problem and your excuse is the new try.

Miscommunications are unmarked graves. Mass incarcerations, the new plantation ways. And, since hash tags and airbrushed shirts are the new justice for dead children, I won't even debate the new slaves.

I whoop my kids in parental ways and have to leave and get my mail going to jail. Police, shoot my kids and get paid leave and money for bail.

Heaven on earth, the new hell. A screenshot, the new proof. Lies, the new truth. Too many kids think they're grown these days, so trashy and shy is the new cute and somehow, the elderly's the new youth.

School, the new nanny. Xbox, the new daddy. Momma, 32 years old, the new granny. Down low is the new plenty for the some of these brothers, so false affection is the new undercover and side chicks are the public's new lover. Then you discover an abortion pill, that's the new rubber.

I used to wonder how a man with excess on his plate will let his homey starve, while a man with next to nothing will carve into his last meal. Friends and family will turn on you quick if you don't pay the past bill, which leaves a stranger to be the one to pray for you and help your ass heal.

Stolen merchandise, the new deal. Gay is the new straight. Stud is the new man. Mr. Bruce Jenner, the new woman of the year and then you have 22 inches, 6 pounds and 2 ounces of virgin Brazilian weave, the new bundle of joy in a mother's hand.

Income tax plans, the new hope. Lord washing my sins away, the new soap. I paid all my bills last week, so I can't take you out to eat, but that's the new broke.

Black pride, the new dope and sex, the new love. And love is hitting that pussy raw from the start, using no plastic raincoat, no latex glove. So what you could do is the new don't. What you would do the new won't like business suits, big belt buckles and badges. Let's not front because that's really the new thug.

Deception, the new grudge. Society, the new judge. They say blood is thicker than water, but blood's the new mud. And mud is the new bullshit your name is drug through while bullshit people are the new strangers, posing as family that say they love you which is the new way of saying, "fuck you."

Bad bitch, the new queen. What's behind you is the new scene. You are awake, but still asleep. So we silence the new scream, making to dream, the new evil. Spell it backwards and I can show you what I mean. To dream is the new evil. And being able to spell it backwards is a black newborn's dream. To live.

The Struggle

Fredrick Douglas, 1857. There is no progress without a struggle.

I am spoken word even when the word is not really spoken. Persistence overcomes resistance so I insist that you listen and bless me even before I sneeze or start choking.

When I open my palms and let poetic psalms slip from the south tip of my tongue remember it's not just the gift of gab I'm trying to give you. There's no progress without a struggle so the struggle is the story I'm telling you I was pushed, pulled, and forced to live through.

A mind once bound by shackles and chains, I've slipped through time like air between the droplets of water in rains to overcome animosity powered by the sin within me. Tattooed on my chest to the left, there's nothing to fear but fear itself so I'm not at all scared of any weapon formed up and thrown against me.

Or the true lies from an enemy that befriends me because my shadow's glow blinds like a welder's arc even when I decide to step out of the lime light. Even if you covered me in black paint and drape me in black clothes then threw me in a black pit that's deeper than the black hole in the black shadows on a pitch black night; even in a Chi-town blackout, drinking black coffee, in a black four-walled crack house, eating burned black rice, while shooting black dice, or flying a black kite out , I'd still step out in the black night frost like a VVS studded black knight wearing black tights with black ice of black Christ around my black neck to shine bright.

My time is right now, and right now is the time I put my right foot forward in a defensive stance. Defending my pride, my integrity, my honor, my morality and anything else that may have been forgotten from any other instances.

I come from crumbs to bricks from bricks to buildings. I lived in the slums in the ghetto around punks, prostitutes, dope dealers, nappy-headed children and many killings.

Still envisioning police brutality beatings from crooked cops that are thieving from a society they once swore to serve and protect. Acting like they shit don't stink, so they use a pistol and pepper spray to try to demand their respect.

Just adding more havoc to the struggle I've preached my sermon to the whole choir about. Meanwhile we have a president whose mind seems to still reside and live in the old retired south.

This is a man that only has conflict and debris flying from the hole in his mouth that will never learn. This was the same man that was in charge when the twin towers burned. And when my people needed help from the weather he was the same man that had his back turned. Then four days later he was the same man that gave a piss poor attempt to act concerned.

It seems like I've struggled my whole life to search for a yellow straight pin needle in a hay stack. But for any other man that has the testicular fortitude to struggle through the contents of my mind it's like searching for a silver stray straw of hay in a needle patch.

I seem to match up words with thoughts and feelings then grab them back in a single snatch to leave the mind in a quiver. I once taught a man to fish but he struggled with the concept so hard, he grabbed the hook and line and threw the reel and rod in the river.

I am that clever nigga up the street with no degree on the grind clean from head to feet with no worries on his mind. I once ran into another from Daytona with a college diploma up shit creek without a paddle, peddling with his hands and feet in the muddy water about to commit a crime.

The struggle is what I recite and preach. The hustle is what I might teach. If I tell you I found a way to beat the struggles of the clan go cut three holes in a white sheet.

Because can't no man outfight me in a battle of wits for knowledge. I may be the only man I know that didn't get educated from struggling for a degree in college.

I got it from what I see in the streets. Young misguided and undecided struggling single mothers on a money hustle selling food stamps to get treats.

That's a struggle. Or ex cons past their second strike getting denied second-rate jobs even when they're above second best on a score card.

That's a struggle. Or getting falsely profiled and muscled down to the ground by a crooked cop's billy club pound even after getting bitten by his hound. That's a struggle.

The price of gas is high. Struggle. The price of sitting in class is high. Struggle. Even the price after getting caught with good grass is high. Struggle. My mind is like that rabid pit bull enraged that broke from a cage and it will never be captured, tamed or in a mussel.

I will stay on the loose. Educating and delegating about recent struggles like the Jena Six, the white tree and what happened when it was draped with a white noose.

Some call me the dark truth. I am pride, power and inspiration. I am the eye of the tiger on any night and the fight. I am determination. I am the absolute last of a dying breed representing a suffering nation.

I'm the look in the eyes of a date-raped victim in the doctor's office with AIDS patiently waiting. I'm the falsely accused, and the miscarried child whose sperm donor is still missing. I am that laid-off father of three with bills like no other that's about to lose his place to live in and no food to cook in the kitchen.

Yet, I still have a mission, a black man pacing full of faith even if some may be still wishing and hoping. I am the pain, sweat and tears from childhood fears and lost dope fiends in the streets steady coping.

And after that, I am the aftermath. I am the struggle. I am the spoken word even when the word is not really spoken.

I'm the sole product of my environment; a living progress still living within the process of the struggle.

Time of Hate

I want you all to listen to the words I speak very carefully and think as I take you back in time and tell a story about the past where sometimes death might have been the only good life after. Back to a time where there was only a dream of happiness and laughter. Back to a time where my people had to call a white man master.

Even the good pastor would have a difficult time keeping his composure preaching about love and laughter, breaking the rapture, and the broken hopes of a life after slavery. Some folks even argue that the countless attempts to capture freedom of these courageous black men and black women was stupidity and not the utmost definitions of bravery.

Now let me tell you a new and true story. The kind of story that consists of an unnatural hate and all its glory.

Can you imagine being shipped off against your natural will like cattle in a field watching the tears and blood spill in reason of a white man's ignorance? Brutalized with whips and chains, shackled and thumb screwed on ships in rains, tormented through the mental state to the brain for frivolous reasons of irrelevance.

Or, how bout, tortured and persecuted for trying to gain intelligence and common sense or learn just anything new. How would you like to be put on an auction block and be sold off as someone's property and there wasn't a damn thing you could say or do?

To be stripped away from all your family and truly have no clue of what life for you was next. And then end up on a white man's plantation under the blazing and scorching hot sun having little or no rest.

Having lashes looking like trees on the backs, and two or three families living out of one shack with big rats and having to sleep on no mats but old clothes rolled up in a small space. All because the white men thought it was a damned disgrace to be born with a black face.

By the seventeenth century Africans were chased and purchased in the slave trade. Bought for twenty-five dollars in Africa and sold for one-fifty in America to the white man was the best profit to be turned and made.

Between 1540 and 1850 there was an estimated 15 million slaves on American soil. That's about 15 million lives of black men AND WOMEN that white men have truly spoiled.

And that's not keeping in mind that over half of the slaves forced on the ships died. My people were hated, cheated and lied to about a freedom they'd never see. But they'd see beatings to death or maybe thirteen knots on a rope around an oak tree.

If on the same plantation, a slave didn't even want to live in the same house as his wife because she might be exploited, persecuted and raped before his own eyes in fright. I wouldn't want to endure the continual misery of seeing her flogged and abused without daring to say a word in her defense in the day or night. If my wife must be exposed to the insults and licentious passions of wicked slave-drivers and overseers, Heaven forbid I should be compelled to witness the sight.

Breeded and treated like wild animals in a dog kennel. What type of shit is that? Singing songs with the highest joy of the deepest sadness while living in a world of the deepest madness.

Tobacco, rice, sugar cane, and cotton were labor intensive. Slaves were in the fields from sunrise to sunset and at harvest time they did an eighteen-hour day and no shortcomings were permissive.

Do you know what the definition of Mulatto is? It's the first mixed children because of the white man's days of white man take anything they wanted like rape. Even Abe's Emancipation Proclamation was undermined and September 23, 1862 was that date.

Three years later, the 13th Amendment was passed...that abolished slavery, but racism and Andrew Johnson's Black Codes were still around to restrict my people at the time. So here is another riddle and rhyme I want to put on your mind.

From the docks off the African coast where they herded up the slaves, and damn near the same path the ships took across the Atlantic's waves, and boarded off is damn near the exact same path hurricanes and **tornadoes** develop and form. Now, I wonder if that's one way a herd of angry black men and black women warn and show their wrath with lightning, thunder and rains of the worst storms.

Let that marinate on your mind and then unwind and think of the unknown time a white slave owner from the north telling one from the south how to control his slaves better. Not with lynching and whippings, but turning my people against themselves. So, look it up, it's outlined in what they call the Willie Lynch Letter. Just remember birds of a feather flock together so they will all rebel in any kind of weather.

And will never have their hopes and dreams and spirits crushed by any of the physical and mental things the white man did at the time. I just want you to remember the depressing times of slavery and moreover after I finish this last rhyme.

Untitled

If you are going to fuck. Go ahead and fuck. But, if you fucking somebody you shouldn't have fucked with in the first place that you can't call when you fucked up, and your number probably ain't even saved in his fucking phone, you know you are a fucking sad fool.

So, you should never try to fuck up someone's life with a lie when yours can easily be crushed, destroyed, and annihilated with just one cry of the half-truth. Something I've learned since the day I grew past youth is that temptation has always been a woman's weapon, and will remain a man's last excuse. It's easier to avoid it than resist it.

So, let me pitch this screwball to you all, I've never viewed dogs chasing or seen any U-Haul racing to catch up behind the back of a hearse. Far from better to worse, you can't take it with you, even your emotions die when you fall cursed, and so every one of you with these hard and sensitive, blue ball feelings might as well just leave them right there at that exact moment that pain hurt.

I don't care if it's your main flirt. Beauty without depth is just decoration. Which is why there are two main reasons why we don't trust people without hesitation; either we don't know them or we do know them by some correlation. Even when a woman tells you what's wrong, it doesn't mean she is singing another sad song for your condemnation but, it means she trusts you. Only your actions can bust you or set and keep strong that foundation.

I mean, any man with wisdom can fool you with an imitation of a clown but there is no clown in town that should be able to fool you by playing the part of a wise man. One of the worst mistakes you could ever make is to get lost in someone that won't even take the time to come find you as if they were your prized fan.

Your vision has to be able to look further than the seeing eyes can to see that not everything faced can be changed, but also, remember that nothing can be changed until it is first faced. So, no longer does God need to grant you the serenity to accept the things you cannot change. Instead, you should change the things you knew you couldn't even accept in the first place.

Born and bred with cursed traits, I was taught to be a man since my birth date and that if you don't sacrifice for what you want, what you want becomes that sacrifice. You have to stay true to yourself…because the lies you tell someone else may just be the tip of the iceberg where it cracks the ice.

Even if it lacks a price and blacks the nights, a memory that doesn't involve you or backs your life ain't worth thinking about. Before the truth can set you free you have to recognize which lies are holding you in bondage as a hostage in a drought that won't let you out.

No matter how much you pout, a single lie discovered is just enough stuff to corrupt and create doubt in every truth you ever had to shout to express. No longer blessed, just full of stress. Life's a mess. Women ain't got no manners, men ain't got no standards. A man loves it when you call him daddy, but will hate you if you call him after sex and tell him he is the daddy and what comes next.

Some will talk all day about side chicks, then talk all night trying to be the dude on the side. That's why some men are deadbeat dads, but excellent step-fathers. You thought your pussy would never falter and would get him to the altar, but your pussy is not divine, it's really deeper than poetry, the most abstract line.

The devil is always in disguise, so you have to be careful who you trust because he was once an angel. The truth can be a tangled web to weave, but the untruths we spread is what leaves us mangled, strung up, hung and strangled while you spiritually swing and dangle.

So the next time you see some people out here seeming to be out here doing well from the most critical angles, it doesn't mean that they're blessed. You should never forget the devil also rewards his people for doing his work, carrying out his quests.

What's Sexy

Some people tend to have this simple misconception that sexy is simply looking like a video trick. So I'm here to answer that crippled deception from the tip of my shriveled-up dick when analyzing this false perception by saying that is really not the only quality of a sexy chick.

And I need you to just excuse my language and French when I'm expressing this because there is a difference between sexy and having sex appeal. Sexy...is more than just hypnotizing bedroom eyes and luscious thick thighs on cocoa butter-smooth legs to feel.

Knowledge and what's in your head is what's real or being able to pay your own bills or just cooking hot meals in an oversized T-shirt while wearing pink house shoes. Sexy...is just something about you. And, don't get me wrong, I'm not trying to out-rule sex appeal, but that's just meant for sex and to give your spouse clues.

I'm talking about sexy...not just about a woman with enough sex appeal, I just want to undress me and let me slide in. Not necessarily a model sized ten with a high chin, but sexy can be a size thick between 120 and 225 thin pounds that could care less about the rest and just lets her pride win.

Sexy...is an internal feeling up to no one man for the stealing because attraction is subjective and can't be analyzed. Sex appeal...is the visual perception of another towards you and you can never know if their vision is paralyzed.

Sexy leaves you to fantasize...not like see-through lingerie, but like how Deep Blu would say a strawberry lush Lolli Pop pile-drives full pouty lips in seductive ways to make you blush on hot summer days.

I'm talking about a high yellow light-skinned caramel brown mocha black sista with a chocolate complexion. A heavy set big-boned curvaceous athletic lean and petite woman that has just as much direction and sex appeal as any other to start my erection.

From the classy happy to be nappy with natural afros and cornrows to the perm pressed fried died and laid to the side or if it's just tied up in a pony tail shows natural beauty outside the club in everyday clothes.

That's sexy. No make-up or fancy weaves to make hair stay up. That's for sex appeal, I'm just going to keep it real and say stuff like some women need to not take up these fake rough deals thinking they're sexy when they really need to chill and get some flip flops and stop struggling to walk in these high heels.

Knowing how to clean and not just straighten up where you live, sexy. Not always having someone babysitting, but instead you're out with your own kids, sexy. And, just looking amazing when you're not trying to even if you know someone's watching behind you, yet you still are as noticeable as a black Queen Nefertiti in Egypt's pyramids, sexy.

I want you to just let me see the natural beauty and who you are on the inside from the outside. Show me your stride. Show me your pride. Show me a part of you that only God can provide that no man could ever judge even if he tried.

Something that could never be denied because sex appeal will only make someone take a second look. That's like telling me the end of a story after I see the cover, so now I don't even have to worry about reading the book.

This could be another deceiving hook or a low blow. Sometimes it's better to build on what works than to try to fix what doesn't. So forget what isn't or what wasn't and let your sexiness show.

And stand up for what you know if you know you are one of the sexiest creatures on this side of creation. You don't have to be Maya Angelou to know why the caged bird sings with elation. But if you can pull off both sexy and sex appeal with no hesitation, which doubles the sensation, you need to stand up and shout because no one can ever resist the temptations of that collaboration.

Living Proof

This is for that child that was forced to take a shortcut through hell just to see that there is a brighter side of heaven all on their own. For that child that was forced behind the shadows of darkness that always thought that hell was a place called home.

I'm living proof. Living proof that one man can make a difference in anyone's life from good words that are trapped behind smiling lips on the tip of any man's tongue. Laughter is God's hands on a troubled world so I'm living proof that even the most depressing sights and sounds can inspire the most joyous songs ever sung.

I'm living proof. Living proof that a black nappy headed boy raised by a single mother in a house full of women in the projects can grow up to become the healthy strong-minded inspirational black man you see before your very eyes. Real eyes are known to realize the truth from real lies so you don't have to live up to be your stereotype because it is possible to take the man out of the hood as well as the hood out of the man and achieve it with pride.

I'll be the first to admit to it. I used to do all my dirty work. I used to steal, talk shit, lie, cheat, and didn't give a damn about any man that crossed me and you could never find me in any man's church.

But, now I'm living proof. Living proof that a man can completely change his life around without selling out and can accept the aid from his woman's helping hand. It's said that it's a man's world but we all know it would be nothing without a woman in his corner to keep him focused and help him take that stand.

I'm living proof. Living proof that a black man can be truthful and faithful to his woman and love her unconditionally without a doubt. We seem to spend so much time looking for the right person to live with... when we need to be looking for the person that we can't live without.

The same thing it took to get her, it's going to take the same thing to keep her. So I'm living proof that men are capable of maintaining that fire that makes everything seem sweeter.

But sometimes breaking up is easier than making up, so I'm living proof that you can still be civilized and friends with your ex and can stay in the same house. You were friends before lovers like sister and brother so go back to being friends so enemies is not the only other option for you to discover.

I'm living proof. Living proof that just because a man has been to jail doesn't make him a caged animal plotting to be a predator upon release. My father's blood runs rampant through me, so I'm living proof that a man can rehabilitate his got damn self and work to be anything he wants to be.

No man should ever judge a book by its cover. So I'm living proof that one can truly respect another.

Ambush

This is the ambush. Dedicated to these sorry ass brothers out here that think that thugging is back in style, but all the while, don't even know how to make a gram push.

The ones that would rather just sit around smoking some damn Kush, enveloped in cannabis smoke, choking to get high, just lazy and living a lie to get by on every night. My question is what's wrong with you? Why does the law have to make a plight to get you before you even try to straighten up and act right?

Instead, you want to walk around sagging and back-talk sassing with your pants hanging half off of your ass like you don't even know its origin. It started as punks and fags showing their true colors in prison that their ass was up for grabs for other inmates to mate and start sticking and licking.

This is the ambush. Even for the brothers that tend to blame that damn Bush that's been in office for the past eight as the main reason they can't get a break in life. Always finding some scapegoat that's white, so instead of schooling or a job you go out and rob the community by selling dope from day to night.

What you need to do is stay to fight to win a better life by that will pay you right from a white-collar hustle. You should already know that there is no progress without a struggle…so the battle is already half won to make your revenue double.

You shouldn't let the trouble you got into in the past ruin and dictate the choices you make in the present for your future plans. Because as long as you can keep your faith in that higher man and not see everything as worthless…in time your blessing will surface and you will see that you do have a fighting chance.

So in case I didn't say it in advance, this is the ambush. Even for the women out there that will try to scam us, thinking their damn puss is going to ram and push us to get them what they want out of life. Baby, I just hope you don't think that on any night…because if you do, you got another thing coming to you that will show you right.

But, I'm just going to blow that right by you because in this world you have to learn from your own mistakes for yourself. Learn what's fact and fake without help so you can truly learn and take the concept of life to earn and make your wealth.

That way you can figure out that you're just breaking your health by trying to play these niggas for their money. All in the club singing independent like it's funny, yet when you go home, you may sit in the corner feeling a bit crummy.

This is the ambush. And even a dummy can figure out that I've examined us as a people and am trying to inject this needle to educate. Apparently it's time for our parents to stop and dedicate their lives to our children and not rely on the school system to teach, relay and relate.

It should never be a debate between parent and child over what's allowed if that child is acting wild. Disciplining is a part of parenting…so you should make it a scary thing that your child fears if they ever get out of line or too hostile.

Beat that ass if you have to. You don't have to worry about any CPS trying to get at you. Because if you do it right…they'd be too frightened of you to try to cross your path to sass you.

So as you can see, this ambush is for everybody from young to old. As a black people, we need to remold ourselves away from that evil stereotypical needle to show the world that our race should have never been stolen and sold.

So we can make our own ambush .

Dreamless Death

From the metaphor of ashes to ashes to the dreamless reality of tears crashing onto a pine box casket being viewed from faceless sunken-eyed masks from six feet above ground level. The flesh of my flesh passing with the breeze from my last breath to death silencing a lifelong crash of dreams or nightmarish struggles is now being covered with dirt, rubble and gravel with the help from a caretaker's wooden shovel.

Ending my battle with fate resurrecting my soul leaving my body's dead weight to decay with the maggots and worms plaguing underneath the withered roses resting on my grave's site. Rest in peace is the epitaph engraved right on the headstone seated alone far from home with in loving memory shown to give a throne to my last days of life.

Making it right on any night for my spirit to become an apparition like a magician and transfer through the dimensions in the heart of the graveyard through the cemetery. Hearing the loud cries while the preacher eulogized over a sarcophagus that was crucified in the Lord's eyes carried tormented dried feelings of depression through the mortuary that will never be outlined in any obituary.

Like they say life's a bitch. So does that necessarily mean that death is her brother? I can't smother the fact that this is the worst of a black curse with a funeral line led by a black hearse filled with black suits and black dresses and a matching black purse working their way to fill the back of the black pews of a black church. So how do I discover if there's a new meaning of a black afterlife that's not black lurking around left that will work for me to uncover?

The phantom of darkness has persecuted my living life, which has turned out to be the deep sleep of the unliving life under a black sky. So more after the moment my eyes close is the very moment my eyes truly open to an everlasting life of afterlife with me waking up to the abstract truth of me no longer living the abstract dreams of a black lie.

My trials and tribulations are the lord's reincarnations of give and take like a chess game the Lord is playing within my subconscious mind's state. So where were my pawns and queen at my time of checkmate?

If I'm the king of my castle in life, should I sacrifice my knight even if the bishop is seduced and corrupted by another queen despite the protection from the rook and my right to live? From ashes to ashes to dust to dust, I want to make sure the steel of my coffin doesn't rust because the reality of this dream turned nightmarish from the reality of evil's lust and was too overwhelming for my Lord and savior to forgive.

Phenomenally living a dream that is very real. Fearing a feeling of fear because fear itself is the only thing to be feared. So dying is not feared because in actuality it's waking up from a comatose state of multiple dreams so the moment fate is tested is truly the moment I wake from rest and live the life that I'm destined to live.

With every bone of my skeletal remains symbolizing the several pains the reverend explains and strains that this is my resurrection and the beginning of new life. Ending the fallacy of a falsified and blemished reality awakening me to a better world completely free from sin and any stress and strife on any given night.

Emotions Unheard Of

I'm feeling as if I'm drowning in the pits of an endless oceanic abyss of circumstantial loneliness and self-pity blinded by that obnoxious beam of delusions of pride and an unwanted dignity. As something sits with me submerged within the still waters pulling me vigorously behind the shadows of the shallows of infidelity, it commits to the sin instilled within me ensuring and empowering itself with trickery making me become my own unknown enemy.

And the swallowing of my own miseries is that spectacle of infamy that floods my lungs from the pain of the wild winds and powerful showers that runs into the gutters and drains. As violent as the furies of hurricanes and cold as the droplets of the drizzling rains, no one understands my pains as I hear the unspoken echoes of my name straining in whispers in subsequent vain.

Even envisioning the irritable flashes of the wrinkled pages and contorted scenes of my biography through a kaleidoscope of broken glass from a shattered mirror makes it harder for me to remember. Even when the tears stop flooding my eyes and are wiped clean, my vision remains distant and still isn't any clearer.

And as the light gets dimmer and darkness nearer... from a faint reflection in the center of the array of chaotic bubbles from my panic I'm captivated in a trance by a cold stare and bleak grin engulfed with sin. Laughing at my tortured soul and blended loss of oxygen with tormented revenge pulling me again towards the end pretending to be a merciful friend as I put up a pointless struggle and descend.

The deafening screams in dreams wake me gagging and choking on the salt water of sweat and fatigue from my own heartbroken pleas on my knees from nightmares. There's nothing to fear but fear itself but I never knew that fear would bring upon with itself its own frightening scares.

Drowning myself in my own tears. Frightened from my own fears. Hearing the lowest decibel of frequencies throb in my ears making the smallest water molecule unstoppable and follicles of unlogical fears powerful and near like a gothic executioner's invincible spear.

They say time is a healer and in all due time all things shall get better. I'm in a storm without an umbrella and freezing without a sweater so I hope the way I feel doesn't last forever and will change in due time with the weather.

Like the weight of a feather, the uncharted depth of this abyss is like a stalling of the free falling with an unknown suspense of a black hole or bottomless pit. I'm lonely. I'm anxious. I'm miserable. Emotionally sick. Just fluttered with a continuous long list of bullshit and emotional conflict.

And now the weight of the crushing water has begun to take its effect. Not repenting my sins, my own lies and ungraciousness and not expressing my loves are just a few of my many troublesome regrets.

My own fatal flaws of twisting emotional laws with no cause are the cause of the fatal jaws that kept my life falling and cursing. The claws from the paws I once saw with the raw grin foresaw those laws and made me withdraw that fatal piece that was flawed from this jigsaw and made me a better person.

Stopped me from being worrisome and stopped me from drowning in my own sins. All I need is for someone to throw me a line. This can't be the life for me, the beginning of the end. I need for God to show me a sign.

Please, Lord; lower your shine so you can help for me to glow. I'm trapped and suspended within the still waters of my own mind drowning and lost and I don't know where to go.

I need someone to come and show me a new love. I need someone to free me from this emotional distress and be the bearer of some new emotions unheard of.

Escape

    Is it possible to find quiet in a world full of thunder? Or even is it possible to just stop hateful actions, for it is love we all must hunger?
    I can't see the truth. I feel as if I'm trapped behind a wall of illusions. Illusions so vague I can't derive any logical conclusions.
    Causing contusions in my mind because I've dreamed that I'm dry, yet standing in the middle of the street in the rain. Could this have the unknown meaning of having a little comfort while truly being overcome by pain?
    Or is this a clue of telling me what's next in our lives? The present cries while the past dies despite the future, which is pre-written yet; I still don't know what lies.
    Could the rain be the tears of all the lost souls that have suffered? Crying all around me to let me know that tears are a relevant feeling I will soon discover?
    My feelings of happiness seem to have disappeared like a sweet smell in the air. I've tried to reminisce myself with that aroma, but for some unexplained reason it just wasn't there.
    I wonder if it's possible to go to a world where there's no sadness or hate. Better yet, I wonder if it's possible to just escape.

Frustration

How do you know when you really love someone? How can you really tell, if in fact, that that person is the only one?

Love is just a man-made word, yet its meaning is a state of mind. So, how exactly do you know when you're with someone you've given it enough time?

Personally I think love should be destined as well as a destination. It should be cherished and rendered through with levels of gradation.

So, now how should I feel? What's the best way for me to find out if your love's real?

People say when you're in love, you know it. But, how do you know it's not just lust and what exactly is the best way to show it?

So, now what should I do? How do I find out if your love is genuine and true?

I am so confused. It's true I have strong feelings for you but I just don't want my feelings to get misused.

In order for me to find out we have to maintain the highest levels of communication. It's the only way to free me from this mental frustration.

Heaven Or Hell

How would you like to go somewhere where hateful faces collide like the tides beat against the sand of the shore? A place where total darkness allures.

How would you like to go to a place where you'll never have rights? A place that gets even hotter every time lightning strikes.

Somewhere so dark you're afraid of that white line because it can take any good word or rhyme, bend it through time and make it cruel and unkind to the unconscious mind.

It's a fiery place, yet it can feel so cold. It's where you will be eternally, mind, body, and soul.

This is a terrible place most if not all dread. It's a place only a select few are sent after they're dead.

How would you like to go somewhere where love, laughter, and beauty will never grow? How would you like to go to Hell, that horrifying fire down below.

Or would you rather go to a place only seen after death and in all dreams; A place of only imaginations and the most beautiful of things.

This is a place beyond the furthest of sight. This is the only place that's full of love and forever bright with light.

It's the only place where you can see the angels sing. This is truly a place of life and good feelings.

And the only fallacy is that it's not reality, because in reality you are never completely free.

And once you're here you can never fall. This is the only place that looks at your petty sins and forgives them all.

How would you like to go to a place that's forever laughter and love? How would you like to go to heaven…. That beautiful place up above.

Hold My Hand

Just listen to me. At this moment in time, I don't want to you to try figure out what's going through my mind, I just need you to hold my hand. I've already put this in God's consoling hands, so I really have no reason to try to control His plan.

Right now, I feel as if my soul is bland or as cold as Klan burning crosses on lawns of church houses between shivers of every winter solstice. The spaces between my fingers were made to lock between yours, and I know this, but tonight is just one of those nights I feel so down out and hopeless.

So, I need you to hold my hand. Rub my back, hug me in your lap, I need you to show this man that, in prayer, it's best to have a heart without words than words without a heart. There's no sound more earsplitting than the sounds of deafening silence, so try this with me as I pray in this quietness for all the suffering to part.

But, before I even start, just know that this has nothing to do with you…I just need my hand to be held. Now, I don't know if some wicked witch has cast her spell; it really doesn't matter like heartless laughter, I just want you to keep this to yourself as if you've never played kiss and tell.

This is my whispered yell that echoes deep inside a tortured soul to let go of the shackles that it's allowed to be tattooed, and tackle the sweetest taboos that I still find myself loving. I need your arms wrapped around me. I have washed up tears about to drown me and I can't survive if I know that somehow there will be more pushing and shoving.

So, while your fingertips are caressing and rubbing, I need to feel the strength and compassion through your lifelines that run like vines with your gentle touch. Your healing hands are Christ-like, more than enough, and are able to soothe whatever cruel nemesis that has made what once was more than smooth more rigid and rough.

I just want you to hold my hand.

Magic Mirror

How does it feel to stare into the eyes of a man that doesn't want to be seen? The eyes in the reflection seem to grow in depth, yet it's truly the only set of eyes, which knows, and understands me.

This figure before me seems faceless and drained to the soul of all its natural life. And as a lifeless tear crawls from the ducts, it's as if it's the first blood shed drawn from the open wound of the most gruesome and feared knife.

Adding to my strife, involuntary facial expressions reveal the depressing oppressions through the eyes of the most tormented man. The swollen eyes, the puffy lips, and the locked jaws are just a few of the many gestures I really don't understand.

I was once told that a man grows stronger the more he suffers and prevails from enduring the most pain. If this is true my strength should have no limits cause I've been though too much trial and tribulation and stress and strain.

So am I to blame? Should I embrace the shame of a life that's too hard and too cold to maintain?

You reap what you sow is what I always hear. It's sort of like looking at an oceanic abyss in a bottomless pit when you notice your own eyes shedding a tear.

So could this be one of my greatest fears? Why do I feel like this? I wonder if this feeling of resentment has ever run through any of my peers.

Ol' Skool's Blues
(song lyrics)

(intro)
Because I know now exactly what I've asked for.
Kept the secrets in my heart
And I will sang this song, oh yes I will
Even if no one sings with me
I said know now what I've asked for
Buried these secrets so deep in my heart
And I will play this tune
Even if this tune doesn't play for me

This is my testimony
Fuck fake fraudulent cronies posing as my homies
So phony with bullshit
It's the brothers you're cool with
Be the main messy ones
Poppin' off at that mouth in your business,
So dig this, they support you for the ignorant,
The foolish, the childish, stupid cruelness the wild shit
Just go ahead and do this
It's the coolness
Cheer on toothless rudeness
If you ever find
Yourself in a bind
Up at any time,
They're useless and gone
Like Nokia phones
I was laid off
No pay out
Rent was due, told to stay out
No way out
Soaking wet in a rain drought
Separating the pain out
The last hired first fired
I used to have a good woman
Now she looks at me as if she's too tired
And may be taking my kid
Like punishment with a wig

I blame the things that I did
Please Lord, forgive sins I lived
I lost sight of myself
Trying to be what I wanted to be for you
Instead of what you need me to
But you know my love was true

(hook)
"This is the blues
The last man hired
The first man fired
Regardless of attitudes
Love done lost and left me
Heart is so heavy
A broke down Chevy Coupe
The alcoholic drinking
Muddy water singing
Back stabbing banging crews
A kid, may have to see it go
The worst damn dream you know
Somehow I'm living, breathing blues"

I'm drinking Brandy and wine
At a hole in the wall
Getting wasted,
Muddy water singing and cryin'
Was banking and buyin'
Now I'm back to standing in line
No experience overqualified
Yea they draining my pride
Got me thinking about
Drugs, violence, drinkin' getting high'
Or faking the crimes
Get loose as a noose
Go hang a few times
With something jiggling and fine
Quarter horse with a banging behind
I'm just looking, good cooking
Wife say she claiming she mine
Maintaining my stride
With a broke down Chevy
Waving at rides
No sense in saving the dyin'

Can't miss my baby's goodbye
Hell yea, it's scathing my mind
Her not being as brave as a lion
Got to have my baby in my world
For the last days of my life
So stop framing the lies
It's like confetti parading my mind
You're lazy and tired
I'm not this is the way to unwind
You're crazy as vines
Get out, get gone , away a few times
Save a few dimes
For the next chick you're layin the pine
And slanging them rhymes

(hook)

    They pleaded the boss' case while I sat in the office space. Told me with a coffin face, you lost this race, get out this place. You and your tools, no longer needed. And to think I was the only fool that took pride in my work, sometimes bleed it till it hurt, and you can believe it. Fired, not laid off. Do not pass go, bet not collect two hundred on the way out.
    At no instance, don't think about unemployment assistance. Forget your bills. Good luck on your meals. I hope that Chevy truck breaks down while shifting gears and one thug steals the two wheels and you overdose on three Advils.
    Take that to the house. Go home to a lost unloving spouse. Give her a douse of your life. Drank that, spit it up, bet not mix it up with sprite. Drown your sorrows in a Jack Daniels Dixie cup and take shots for the rest of the night, with tears clouding sight.
    Wave goodbye to whatever life you wanted to have. The Chevy broke, so call one of those fake phony friends to see if they will pick you up to cope with drunken laughs.

Prisoner

I am a prisoner living within my own mind
Trapped behind unreal walls of aggression
And steel bars of depression....
Solitary confinement.....
Scratching days
off of gray chipped bricks
that sit in my thoughts that are timeless
where the hatch marks are never in alignment....
So I now make it my solitary assignment
to divide the space-time continuum
and live in my own millennium
dividing space and time....
And as I now began to win the race within my mind
I find a pace at which I still feel alive...
I am free.

Some say I should see justice in the mind's penitentiary...
And I do.....it's just us.....

Questioning Love

When I had too many…I admit…I would only love one. And when I only had one, as you can guess, I would love too many.

So, it's clear to see that women are not my specialty. But still…they are very special to me.

Now, I know some history is based upon truth…but most is also based upon deception. So if a woman ever said I didn't love her…that was only her perception.

Now, it's not that I'm addicted to sex. Truth of the matter is…I'm addicted to women. Most of them know the truth. But others think that that truth is what I'm really pretending.

Huh, if the many never stepped up and approached me…I guarantee…I'd have no problem loving just one. But because I have no problem loving too many…that one that just approached me…seems to feel lost in the fun.

It's not that I'm cold and heartless. That's not even scratching the surface. I have feelings for every last one of them…even if some of them think my love is worthless.

I was once asked if a man can possibly be in love with two women. And I replied yeah…I don't see why not. Then they asked me if a woman can be in love with two men. And that was a question where the answer I had a little doubt.

I know that women feel deeper than men and they seem to let everything go and put in their all. Meanwhile, most men just put in enough to please her and make her smile…thinking if they do just enough that it would stand tall.

Just playing the game to the fullest by doing everything right with good conversation calling each other pet names. Now, sincerity might be riding on that woman's side…but the entire time, that man's ulterior motive is to get up in that "wet thang."

So as you can see, women are not my specialty. But still…they are very special to me. When I had too many, I would only love one. And when I only had one, I would love too many. But that never stopped them from loving me.

Reflection

He looked me right in the eyes as if he could see right through my disguise to a bitter and tortured soul. And after that, I couldn't even control my gestures to even look back at his face. I felt shame…with no one to try to release or place the stress of blame on but myself. Even he knew I needed help. I still felt his staring gaze at my slumped over position as I peeped through this maze in my peripheral vision at his tears. Many times, over the years, I had confided in him about most of my fears, but this was probably the very first time that I believed that his gears were rusted from this melancholic atmosphere. And although I knew that he would always be the first and last to cheer or support me in any way, it seemed like this day was different…as if he had, maybe, lost his passion. We both had this understanding that joy and happiness was never meant to be everlasting since even the Bible states that weeping may last for the night, but at first light, a shout of joy comes in the morning. But, now, I don't think he knows what to believe since he told me that there's even times he would seem to grieve at breakfast, still in mourning, from the weeping of the night before. I just wish I could help my friend. I just wish we could show each other what's in store and that it's ok to play in the rain because it can possibly make you not realize that pain you just endured within a storm. He even said that sometimes cold nights in an empty bed would keep him more warm than the intimacy of multiple women he could have at his discretion. The connection he once had with the love of his life was lost. This was a feeling I could relate to like a candle's flame to a moth, wanting to be near it at all cost, knowing that that flame of resentment, rejection, and regret still burned the flesh and would possibly never be blown out. So, in utter silence, disregarding that surrounding violence, we just sit and stare at each other. Telling old ghost stories, envisioning distance memories of faraway lovers we once wanted to have. This actually made me laugh as a smile crept on his face. And, that was the very moment I knew that we were one of the same that understood each other's case.

Sabotage

It's no longer a perfectly imperfect disguise through guilty eyes that I've become a victim of my own demise. Camouflaged through pixelated images of fabricated truths, bent through youthful light years of a mirage, I've become my own sabotage hidden in the murky dimness within this wasted garage.

I pray this is my last fault. Seems like with each valiant effort to decipher and decode or pick the lock on the cash vault, whatever that is crass stalks and preys on me faster and I end up falling off the steeple's ladder, face down in my own fecal matter on the asphalt.

For some reason I just can't stop. It seems I just continue to sprint past halt to a familiar figure outlining another who has chalk when I near the decaying deconstruction of my own life. I sit aside myself by myself with a knife…watching me, provocatively, through bifocal lenses, unknowingly priding myself on breaking down my own defenses with the final blade toward my spinal cord on each and every plight.

So on each and every other night I blame the other's sight for looking at the other broken shards of another's kaleidoscope instead of the other visions perceived that might have hope to see through another's reflection in another's mirror. All of this change just doesn't make any sense as it gets nearer. I've lost touch with my roots like Wyclef and, although I see in high def., my perception still isn't any clearer.

Success doesn't lead to happiness, but happiness leads to success. I've even poisoned the next in this process by burying the wounded and praising the dead before they were ever laid to rest.

Creating a spiritual unrest from the forgotten souls it protects as they rot and decay with the skeletal remains after worms and maggots have ripped and torn the flesh from the bones while they lay like sardines in casket closets. I am the stench of ungraciousness and grief from hidden love affairs with silver hairs that can leak from the broken valves of brass faucets.

A phony composite sketch drawn from a computer glitch in the DA's office, running a scam to set up the very face that reflects my own image of a lying snitch seen in a *trench* through tinted glass. I spoil milk and honey paid for with counterfeit money, then stutter while I consume my own bread and butter after the expiration date has already passed.

I am my worst enemy making up true lies, genuinely derived from the sin in me, forcing my reflection to innocently pretend to be the next of kin to me or at least, timidly, be another backstabbing friend of me waiting to gag my clone or the twin of me with a chloroform rag in the murky dimness within this wasted garage.

    I am the reason things go wrong like tears in a joyous song that can't be camouflaged on the surface. I create my own destruction within my life to make life seem worthless, cutting my own brake lines before long half-awake drives into a mirage on late nights. But it's never on purpose. Sabotage.

Scrambled Thoughts

How can I put into words how I really feel sometimes? What combination of words can be formed to represent certain emotions, and moreover, is it always possible to make it all rhyme?

I mean, sometimes I feel as if the world and all its powers are against me. What did I do to deserve this? Why can't I live happy and free?

Every time I think I'm doing right, everything always seems to go wrong. If my life were music every other track would be another disturbing and confusing song.

For some reason it's hard for me to open up to people and let them know what's really on my mind. I don't know, I guess I hope the pain would just fade away with the time.

And even if it does, it often finds a way to resurface itself. And just like any other time I'm at a lost for words when I could really use a little help.

I know I'm not alone and everyone has their own troubles, but I'm talking about me right now and it's as if all my troubles have doubled.

I know I'm not the only one going through trial and tribulation, but shit, am I being punished for molding myself out to be my own creation?

Does anyone out there truly comprehend how I feel? Have experienced and been through, for lack of better words, bullshit, that you don't know what to believe or what's really real?

Maybe it's just me. But, who gives a fuck? I'm the writer and I can say what I want to say. I can curse and put down the world, but that's now the vibe I'm trying to get out today.

I just want to be heard. And speak on behalf of all the people who may feel the same sometimes and let the others hear the word.

I don't know what to say. Maybe I'm just blowing off a little steam. It's just like I'm living the life of my own nightmarish dream.

Shackled

To the unheard, regretful cries from push and shove, tell me how a life with the most perfect imperfections of love can come to this. Anguish. Conversing hollow poetry from a shattered soul's language.

It seems like all of a sudden, with no glutton for tenderness, I was handed hate. So, now I just lay like a battered carcass in this scattered darkness, lost in transition in a manic state.

And only fear and panic wake me to see that I'm still alive to see the reflections of a soul-mate that has sold their soul a long time ago. I no longer have a chained body with a free mind. Instead, my thoughts of freedom are in timeless shackles with a bruised body and no help to find.

I want to delete this. I can longer keep these secrets.

A bruise covered with a sweet kiss doesn't relinquish the agony that unfolds consequently from wrath. And it's sad that underneath this math, the numbers still don't equate up to a righteous path.

I didn't know I could bleed. And it seems like the only chances I took to analyze my own life was in times of need.

I guess chasing a dream can be seen as running from reality. But, I've never had that type of mentality. My chaos not only exists outside and around me, but the fatality of chaos also coexists within me.

So how can I escape? With shackled hands, a chained mind, and a tackled body, thoughts of freedom from this anguish are rowdy in rewind as my life seems to be in fast-forward throughout time.

I've chained and shackled my mind to a delusional ghost that acts like a jackal that coasts and haunts me, inconspicuously. I've allowed it to stow away with the key as it drags me on the heels of its two swollen feet. And just like an apparition of its kind, I can only drift behind like some animated dead with a voice of a thousand that tread with no tongues to speak.

A prisoner…trapped within the fiberglass walls of my own romantic illusions. And I can only see my own antics with inevitable conclusions from the reflections of a spirit without a soul whose essence has multiple contusions.

Bruised…beaten down and misused, the inner enemy within me has grasped the sin in me and manipulated any transgressions in the vicinity of righteousness and used it as a weapon of torment. So who's the victim? I can only blame myself because I've allowed this nemesis from Genesis to not lay dormant.

Like a storm vent, it seems as if I'm permanently open like a warm trench to any trash and debris that may be carried with any bleeding currents of pain. My soul is shackled and chained. My spirit is tackled and drained. And I don't believe any soothing rains could ever wash my hands and keep them from being crackled and stained.

It seems as if I've lost sight of the man I used to be. Like a child in a basement, I've become complacent and too familiar with the emotional darkness that surrounds my unanimated carcass.

Even when I glance towards my dissipated and heartless reflection upon glass I can't surpass the tears that drown my masked soul. I don't even know why I even bother. Maybe I should just come to terms and accept the fact that I am the son of a father who has lost control by somehow manifesting a misery from a history untold.

So, now I just sit here in mystery saturating my own flesh because I'm overwhelmed by the tests of life. I was once told that real men don't cry through the night and real men don't try to get it right, but I've been able to win gunfights with a knife.

I can't be told of the things other folks say that real men can't or won't do. I've cried. I've prayed. I've tried. I've stayed. I've died. I've slaved. Confided and gave. Been lied to and betrayed. But, now it seems as if I can only wave, "hi" and "bye", like a parade, as I lie shackled with pride in a grave.

Solitary Entrapment

　　I feel lost and stuck behind these shallow delusional walls of an optimistic oppression from an alternate unparalleled realm. Behind the chipped painted bricks and cold steel of a locked cell in my own mind living a sudden hell that makes me question the very legality of existence of my own self.

　　With me engaging in heated battles opposing the forces hot enough to melt the very fabric of any tactical moves that are prone to prevail without any outside help from infiltrators and intruders. Whether from haters or wrongdoers, steady shakers or slow movers, I feel secluded and confined without any generative maneuvers away from the murky dimness of my own mind in an unusual and solitary sewer.

　　Where the weather only goes from cooler to cold freezing the ice tipped mold of an iceberg on a wet winter night that can chill frostbite and refrigerate hypothermic conditions. My thoughts are numb and frigid. Just crippled from the collage of mirages corrupting my soul and camouflaging the wildness within my life blinding my own visions.

　　Faced with too many decisions and living a life that I know shouldn't be living. I want to be ridden of any sinister thoughts and be given a second look on life to find any hidden strife I might be able to rectify on any given night.

　　I want total sanctuary. I want my soul to be baptized in pure goodness…that won't capsize if I took this gift of purity and still found a way to unwrap lies that were semi-ruthless.

　　I want to be able to find refuge in my own mind. And not live like a toothless python in an insane asylum with no eyes that couldn't bite on and paralyze its own prey, so I starve even more as my body constricts and winds and my thoughts stiffen up my spine from night to day.

　　I need more justification and meaning for my life. I'm confused and conflicted. Feel misused and constricted. Laid slain from these wicked tools of conviction with whiplash incision to my intellect clouding my visions for my definite provisions for maintaining an existence that's not lived by the blade of the knife.

　　I want out. To break the chains and the shackles of tyranny from my sanity restricting me from the life I deserve to live. I need to be released from this tenacious enemy of my own mind and be resilient to emancipate me from this cage so I can feel the joys in life a good man deserves to feel.

I need to be true and stay real to the most important person in my life. Myself.

Spiritually Dehydrated

This is my untold story. I was raised by the slums, gamed by the streets, living the not-so-unique life where just about everything unfolds to be your main worry.

With snotty-nosed kids scurrying along the playground streets burying their sweet sorrows into the superficial happiness of a world they not yet know the truth about. Being inside the house before momma's loud shout or the streetlights popped out into the murky dimness lived the silhouette of an untold life where sin is corrupting the lost souls of the unforgiving, living their life on the end of a rattlesnake's lying hiss.

So now I'm here standing in the midst of hollow tears raining into shallow rivers of fears and loneliness from immoral clouds of despair generating ferocious currents of true lies and animosity. Carrying me into another realm engulfed with a complete and ritualistic hypocrisy.

Something that seems not to be at all a plot for me to be living my life behind the tormented eyes of a reflection that's out for me lying behind the shattered scenes in the mirror. Having no control, watching my own self fade and disappear, as the goodness in me is wiped clearer.

The eyes are the gateway to the soul. The reflection's eyes grow in depth and shed tears from foreseeing that there is a greater darkness growing even nearer that no man could ever control and console.

So now I'm a runny nose running those streets growing up seeking out a life for me that's free from man's known crime. Just remember it's hard to get that monkey off your back when that monkey stands on your shoulders and starts to tickle your mind with a tail that paralyzes your spine.

And even at the drop of a dime it can blind you and turn back the hands of time making me reiterate that first line. It's hard to get that monkey off your back. It never relaxes or eases the tensions so if in the event that you do shake it free that struggle results in deep wounds from that monkey's scratch.

And gushing from that laceration are all my bodily fluids that have quenched my emotional being. Leaving me mentally and spiritually dehydrated.

Suicide

His palms are moist, knees are weak, and voice is hoarse from screaming and arguing with this consciences choice bothering and hollering at him about the destiny of his own fate. The bones in his body collide and feel as if they are going to collapse like a frail crate from the nervousness and high anticipation of the Lord answering his prayer that he prays for Him his soul to take.

But on the surface while he is still awake he looks calm like he is patiently waiting for any obstacle or any weapon that is formed against him. Only this time he is afraid that that weapon will prosper and will cost him his eternal life as it grows slim from deep within him.

He wants to live without strife but on this night he feels that this decision is just right. Whether with sin or pride or die within a lie trying to penetrate the rogue renegade or feelings in the shade of complicated circumstances. There is something still in the way guiding him away from that guiding light and he doesn't give a fuck whether it's wrong or right because he is prepared to take those chances.

Because he's had his life strangled by the iron fists of oppression, which has been a deep lesson on depression that's made him keep pressing on instead of re-resting on thoughts that kept him stressing.

But now it's different. Now, he knows that life is still a bitch. And since death is her brother, he no longer feels guilty about his choice but innocent, so he really doesn't give a shit.

Cause for as long as he can remember he has been a usual suspect that's a victim of circumstance, just guilty until proven innocent by association. His mind's in mayhem, teeth are gritting, pulse is racing, and he is tired of facing the good book's scriptures embedded and carved between his temples, because the understanding of them have never been too simple. Knowing that the stone the village rejected is the same stone that God put at the top of his temple.

But his soul is lost and trapped in the crevices of a wrinkle in time. Chaos and anarchy is only a few of the tormented states situated at the top of his mind.

And just at the very moment he thought there was nothing left. He slipped his head through the noose and kicked the chair from under him. He hung himself.

The Glass Eye

As you know, all my life, I've prayed for others and not ever have I really prayed for myself. I don't know why, but maybe in the back of my mind, I thought I was never deserving of God's graces, so I went about my life, by myself, trying to receive his blessings without anyone's help.

I guess I figured only I can control my health, my well being and wealth and anything else that I have no control over was exactly what it was; something that I have no control over.

The brightest future will always be based on a forgotten dark past; after all, you can't go on successfully in life until you let go old mistakes, sorrows, and headaches and fiascos, so the pursuit of happiness can be sought after and consoled to last.

When the door of happiness closes, soon after, another door opens. But, often times, we look so long at the closed door that we don't even see the new one which has been opened for us and what person behind it has spoken.

I know that enough joking and laughter can cause a heart to be fine and working, enough pain and hurt can cause it to be broken, and enough tears can saturate and stain it. A person can only look through their own eyes into their soul to see mistakes and search for a true love and pray to maintain it.

Never in my life have I prayed for miracles. I've always hoped that miracles prayed for us. Because when you're amongst God and fear him only... the rest of the world is just dust.

The words I speak are not meant to be unjust, they're only spoken for God's sake and to heal me and reveal me to the unseen. Sometimes it feels as if I've been living my nightmare all my life...so I'm now just trying to be a part of someone else's dream.

And that's where you'll find me...in the midst of the dreams. And you'll never have to remind me, because I at least know I that I have lived a life of ambition and Godly things.

Just like they say, when it rains it pours...but when a poor man reins all the crops are watered. Some people tend to forget that Eve in the Garden of Eden was made from Adam's rib, but she was also the king of all king's daughter.

But destiny holds what the Bible unfolds. And even though I never chose to read it, I was softly told there's no pleasure without pain and no progress without a struggle. It's true I am the master of my fate and the captain of my soul... but Christ is the king of my castle which makes me a peasant at his throne.

So I am only to blame, I point no fingers and tell no lies. I have to deal with the shame with lost dignity and pride.

There have been a lot of times that I thought to myself that maybe I should have done this, or should have done that. Truth is, I done what I thought I needed to do. That's all I have ever done because in my life there has been no time for second guessing. It's either yes or no, you're damned if you do, damned if you don't; I'd have time later to worry about regrets or any outcomes to be stressing.

While watching with a glass eye those with more getting more given to them, and those with less being stripped of the little they have. I was born into a world that has no mercy for the weak that has no blueprint to a good life and no map down the right path.

With my glass eye, I see my own wrath through my reflection when I stare into the eyes of a tormented man glancing at a two-way mirror. I know my world should be full of fun and laughs, yet the warmth from my breath on the glass makes my vision hard to pass and even when wiped clean my vision is distant and isn't any clearer.

The fear of God is instilled within me, so I ask of you to pray for me. Help me rid the sin in me and keep it away from me.

Time Will Heal

I was once told that time will heal. And even though my mind sits still, I know that even the Bible states that there is a time to kill. It's just that being stuck behind ideal pressures of pine and steel makes the crime just feel more sublime and real.

I'm just trying to feel what I once felt when I was searching to find a deal, like the kind of meal designed with skill to refine and fulfill. I mean, sometimes I feel as blind as drills combined with chills that can destroy the spine and heel of mankind for thrills.

But, for now, I'll just unwind and chill, declining pills, blowing smoke from behind my gills while this defying quill entwines and spills the ink that binds and seals. So, while my mind is still waiting for the divine to reveal His kind of will, I hope and pray that time will heal this sign of ill before it's finally peeled or crushed by grinding wheels.

I sit astride the sill as I look to the sky and kneel, then cry and squeal like I'm in a courtroom where they try to steal, then lie and appeal the story of a dying Till. And, honestly, I'll climb a hill just to watch this movie, outside the mill for ninety bills, and tagline the reel as I prime the grill.

I really hope and pray that time repeals my mind and my heart heals with time. I feel that I'm so destined for greatness that nothing steel or pine, whether real or designed, can kill my vibe or conceal my shine.

I have meat on the grill with wine. I call it "chill and swine;" and this meal is mine. I'm willing to poison with pills or pride or break heels and spines for any deals or and tries of stealing my healing highs.

Even if there is a scab left to peel behind, I'd still feel alive, fulfilled and thrived as I take the wheel and drive my life to place of great thrill and surprise. I reveal and disguise appealing the lines that can refill the wise and instill the blind to chill and ride in a teal-lined Seville designed to squeal outside or another automobile with spies.

As a matter of fact, even if I was in Brazil or Versailles, with eels or flies, I could heal the times of ill and demise with surreal supplies of God's grace and skill in my eyes. I now write the bills for crimes and I will survive regardless of whether the ideals of time will heal my mind. But, let us not forget that God has always been real and divine with His will in time.

To Whom It May Concern

For as long as can remember I've been alone on or around days that feel the absolute worst to be alone. I feel as if I'm a lost prisoner forgotten in solitary confinement forced to oversee a falsified, delusional clone portray me and live my life as my own.

Now, let me see if I can explain this. Behind these shallow walls, true love is recognized, meanwhile, the outer nemesis misuses and manipulates even the simplest single kiss.

Shit, even teardrops have stained various chapters of the pages of my endless and confusing story. No set conclusions can be derived from the coded illusions seen and even the frivolous irrelevancies seem to make me worry.

As a male, it's hell for me to tell the tale of what prevails as life's trials and tribulations unveil secluded between the layers of a cryptic shell, but easy to dwell as an infidel in a similar cell that's prone to fail in a parallel realm.

It's been like an entertaining game of a tormented reign of shame and pain, with some range of fame, but no one to blame, making me insane in the brain from the same game of arrange and exchange the strange pains and gains obtained in order to maintain a life that's only domain is an unbroken chain that will forever remain without my name spoken in vain.

Simplicity is the dividing line between eloquence and plainness. But it's a test of time to find that dividing line between painful and painless.

I know it may be hard for you to understand or withstand the different commands that I ran that landed in your head and hands. But this is the way I feel. I feel if I can stand in the middle of the land in demand with sweat from my glands from a large pan of commands and understand everything, I should be able to stand in that same land and be in command without having to demand anything.

I don't know, I guess it's just another lesson learned like fire will burn and money has to be earned. Me feeling the way I feel is for all and anybody to observe and to whom it may concern.

Unheard Cries

I feel as if I was born into a world that has no mercy for the weak. And now I'm a victim of loneliness and sometimes I just can't speak.

Being stuck behind the shadows of a bottomless pit keeps my life falling. And I'm always the last one to hear when love's calling.

Thoughts of fear sometimes override my thoughts and console my mind. Someone I can truly love and trust is too hard to find.

And for that, sometimes people always find a way to shun me and feed off of my sorrows. Now I wish I could have someone else's life to live or borrow.

Even if it were tomorrow as I looked back over my life I've realized I shed too many tears. Much aggression, depression, and thoughtless fears.

When I speak my peace no one ever really tries to listen. Yet, when I oppose the forces of human nature hate's already arisen.

I want you to truly listen to the words I speak because it seems as if I'm drowning in a sea of lies and ungraciousness. I've never peeked over the top to experience true happiness.

So, now I wonder how my life came to this. I'm the first to get dissed but the last to get kissed.

It seems as if every time I think I love someone with my sixth sense I hear good-byes. As a result I think I'm the only one with unheard cries.

Message to my Daughter

A message to my daughter
Pearls of wisdom from fathers
That never received the chance to see their child's life grow any further
From trials and tribulations and temptations that life will bring
You are the purest innocence and why the caged bird sings
My greatest sacrifice is my life for you to live
Your mother would do the same thing, I'm just being real
I will bleed for you to heal
I will burn for you to chill
I would make a deal for my soul so you could have your last meal
To protect and provide
You can confess and confide
Anything you need to tell your parents about sex and the lies
Doing my best I will try
Your every wish is my command
I fall down to my knees every night just for you to sit or stand
No precious jewels on this earth
Could ever stand to your worth
If some man cause you some hurt
I would knock his dick in the dirt
Cause you're my joy and my pain
My sunny days and the rain
You are the fuel to my soul
Igniting my whole spirit's flame
The things I missed, you will have
If out of reach, I will grab
Turn all sadness to laughs
Nothing but treasures, no trash
At your origin I was pouring gin
Sipping it with a horny friend
Holding thoughts like a storage bin
With no money to store or spend
At your birth, I was born again
Like an eagle to soar again
Now I feel like I've scored a win
Through your mom in a world of sin
On a scale, you are more than ten

With your life as you learn and grin
I am your father, yes, more than kin
Never ever your dormant friend
What I do is lay down my life for you
Baby girl you are worth the end
You can breathe while I suffocate
Wouldn't have it no other way
My love for you is oh so great
And my life, you resuscitate
Having you was a gust of fate
You were born just as plush as cakes
And I stood just as tough as clay
You cleansed me and wiped the dust away

Enough

I've had enough and I just can't take it no more. I've heard enough tough lies and seen enough rough cries in disguise just enough times to make me wonder if there really is enough love to give. If there's really even enough to live for because more than enough times I've had to satisfy more than enough people with less than enough lies and be with one woman but be more than enough seductive that also provides.

I've had enough. Even in my dreams I see enough stuff like other black women that refuse to believe us black men can achieve the good life to be living without doing enough sinning or at least achieve enough out of life worth living for. Women say please us and at the same time enough of them deceive us with enough other men. yet in still, enough of them still perceive us as the grinning whore.

Pretending as though enough fortune and fame takes the place of enough education and schooling. Or that enough torture and shame ensure enough strength lies deep within enough of those men that have been through enough fighting and dueling.

I've had enough. I see lust is to be fluffed and plush like deluxe pillows and love is to be crushed and can't seem be thrown out of enough windows so there is really not enough love to even care about. We try so hard to find enough people to live with when we really need to try to find that one person in life with enough love within them we just can't live without.

Someone that won't doubt that enough love has been given out without enough reasonable doubt because I now refuse to put up with more than enough of the madness. I've seen enough jealousy throughout life and it's only cute for so long so just enough drama could have you alone at home drowning in a sea of enough of your own sadness.

And I had this on my mind for a more than enough times so I'm glad this has come to an end. Loose lips sink battleships so since you can't seem tell enough friends so much stuff about us and what we go through, tell them I can't seem to put enough space between us since I've found me a new friend to commit to.

Someone that will sit through more than enough of a boring movie even if it makes us woozy and will do me more than enough times through the morning noon and night. Someone that will try to take enough of my wrongs and help me to make enough of them all to the right.

I just can't get enough. Enough of good love. Enough of good hugs. And more than enough good mental stimulation. Even if we cuss, fuss and fight all night Jesus is still there with us more than enough times to make it right cause we are still together on bended knee praying for enough salvation.

Enough inspiration. Even if love was a sin it she would be just enough to make me fall into those hands of temptation.

I just can't hold her enough. I can't console her enough. Even if I added it up enough of her plus enough of me makes us more than enough complete.

Something that's so unique even though life is a game and gamble so I don't mind if she wins more than enough times or even if she bluffed. So to contradict some of the stuff said at the beginning, her love is something special, and I just can't get enough.

For Better or Worse

Now, let me first start off by saying it was all well worth it. As we stood across from each other, proudly, picture perfect, and took a second good look, the pastor read loudly, as if the scripture surfaced out of the good book, and said for better or for worse. Now, they say birds of a feather will always flock together, but there really was no way of telling whether you would need something like a Bill Cosby sweater to fly in this cold weather or even if a few of those fucking feathers were plucked and cursed.

I don't know, maybe I just wish that I could wake to yesterday, tomorrow, but with today's lessons of sorrow because it seems too much jealous and hurt left us living so much in false perceptions of reality that it made it too damn easy to not relieve disputes. And even after being raped of laughter with deception and molested with the fake chapters of progression, you were impregnated faster with so many lies and indiscretion from "others" and the cavities of their false deceiving tooth…that it became impossible for you to actually make love and consummate with your own lover to possibly conceive the truth.

Instead you miscarried information and aborted the facts and believed a group of people that freely seduced and sexed in lifeboats like horny teenage misfits that are lost at sea on Christmas. Whatever happens between a husband and wife, whether fact or fictitious, has never been anyone's goddamn business. That way, even with a pocket full of constant change, in the fourth quarter of the game, with a dime sack and penny loafers on, not even Jack Nicholson could have cents this. There is no quick fix. It wasn't even a temptation to put any random man or mistress of any sort on the bottom of our wish list, because sex without an emotional connection is really just masturbation with the help of a witness.

So get this. I will be the first to admit this, that this seed was planted in the dark out of shear curiosity, and not even two hoes with shovels in the Garden of Eden could dig this dirt to try to rake up your worth. It's just that things sometimes seemed so malicious and vicious that even if we saw them at the park, Mariah wouldn't Carey chocolate Kisses or even picnic to shoot a Canon for a Kodak to flash delight into the heartless. So, picture it. You once ignited a burning sensation in my soul, so I practiced what I preached to set flames to coal and I couldn't get enough of your love, baby. A fire could not Barry White into the darkness.

Putting everything into compartments that were violent, I even got on bended knee, taking my phone off of silent, to give your heart just the vibrant ring you wanted to hear about during struggles. And even if you left to a place far away and addressed this man's lost love right, as a woman, you could not ever miss me, even if I was in my own space in another city in a burning shuttle. You're better off drinking three bottles of whiskey with four packs of cigarettes, blowing smoke in obscuring bubbles during huddles, because now, I don't care about shit. I'm just pissed, and yes, as you can guess, just like a dope fiend drinking codeine with a bladder infection after the best weed smoking session at a random drug test…urine trouble.

Because my love for you. Damn, my love for you. Wow, my…love…for…you…was not messing up, but speaking, curing stumbles, and and and st st st stutters, whispering through the chaotic clutter just to calm you because talking louder just means you don't speak in volumes, even when you were skipping, when you were skipping, when you were skipping, when you were tripping and falling for shit not worth mentioning that stalled you and caused you to fall through cracks in life that was supposed to be left behind you. Well, let me remind you. Let me remind you. Let me remind you that the past cannot hunt you if you live in the present moment and hide in the future and not allow it to seek or find you.

That's like a starving and hungry, malnutritioned clock that stopped to time you eating while it goes back four seconds…tock, tick, tock, tick. And in that time I been learned my lessons. Here I am, with a phone and no numbers calculated to do simple arithmetic, counting my blessings on scratch paper, hoping and praying to soothe the simplest itch, thinking you were the most fond of me. Even without children, I once stayed all up in the wee hour night, praying to the father, wondering where the son went…and then it dawned on me.

(Aaachoo)(Bless you) thanks, but please…try doing what I did for you by blessing me before I sneeze. And I've never been a rooky, my queen, but I have to get this off of my chess. I feel like my stalemate was just in check and pawned on the king in front of a bishop that knight just to throw salt in the wound. But before you, remember, I was that soldier with a hot jalapeno chip on my shoulder who survived mustard gas and pepper spray in a spicy jungle full of Basil and Oregano leaves…a seasoned veteran; a savage with cabbage, better than the average. Even if you added it up and divided sum by the number added, well, I hope you know this equals what I mean.

I loved you inside and in between, meaning everything on the outside was just cosmetic. So to hell with Estee Lauder's daughters; I never wanted to be L'Oreal's gal or Ms. Maybelline's eye make up your foundation and base with every blush put on your face. You didn't have to mascara (mask error) or shadow imperfections and blemishes; I blend perfectly with you like earth tones of powder in any case.

And, no power to be traced or amount of money proposed would make me marry Kay because of the way you used to lick up and down my lip-stick, you were my comforter everyday with brush strokes in Bare Escentuals, between the sheets, and you didn't even need sheets because I was your cover, girl. Your cosmetic laptop; a true MAC in a lover's world. Making sure you received the best concealer + treatment. Don't worry about where the heat went. I became your relaxer, no lye. Conditioning us to be weaved together and be wrapped in a fashion; no style could be tried to get a better reaction. Even if there was no air for a breeze or too much moisture in the seas... blow dry, because we were colorful, dark and lovely, so alive, happy to be nappy, afro-centric, and even if the hair was turning grey, we'd just Revlon in it, laugh, go pick it, and in every grey we lived...we lived in grey...no color, no dye.

And from birth on this earth, like Marley with hope, pride, no woman, no cry, I was a born slave of your love that took hair-splitting lashes and hair-splitting lashes...for your hair and splitting lashes. Suppressed with nails and chains and shackles and whips... for your chains and nails and shackles and whips until I was hysterical. Listen, I lived off of nothing but quick sandwiches with one strip from a head of lettuce and miracle whip; it was unbearable. And even in quicksand, which made it more terrible, the head would do nothing but lettuce strip, and for you, I was whipped to perform miracles.

And eventually a steady drip of water bore a hole in this rock just as much as the glide in your stride, the dip in your hip, butt in our strut and pep in your step can wear and pop a hole in your sock, and though very hot, I kept very cool, and I admit, it caused some hurt. I earned my stripes, yelling like a pissed off, convicted felon that could pause and numb hurt, but still comes first; like a convict, freshly dressed in a pressed all-star chuck tailored suit after having a discussion behind 16 bars in a song...converse.

And there's never been a reason for me to try to remember some of the worst days or the definite anniversary of when we got together...because I have yet to run across an almanac, a calendar, or scheduler that can treasure a definite date on infinity or eternity, and surely not forever.

But, I know that things change. And since there's a penny for your thoughts, it won't ever make sense when I can't put my two cents in it. The energy that once surged and bolted between us was ecstatic like lightning, so definite, but it wouldn't last, not even *with* help. I mean sometimes, I didn't even care if it was Easter; I became as hot as a ten-thousand watt kilometer and wanted to use a heater to arrest even the Energizer Bunny and charge it with battery and death by electrocution on a fry day until it melts, just because the electricity that sparked between us just couldn't keep current and properly conduct itself; shockingly, not even barely for unfit health.

And though, it felt like a thick belt that had merely left a big welt on me, I was living high in Death Valley, I still loved you…for better or for worse. And there was no pressure at first since we were on the same page, but while my words were like God's word in the Bible, red with rage in a librarian's alley of hurt, your matchbook was struck and either on fire or burnt, and was barely being held up by the blazing tether of your purse.

And whether it hurts me or not, backstabbed with a knife to being to shot and scarred for life, I still laid with you in the cut like stitches. And, I hope I'm not digging too deep, I'm just scratching the surface on purpose when it itches, but we used to dig each other so much. Yet, it's now worthless and seems like we are stuck in the dirt with shovels, trapped from the cave in of our own ditches.

I mean, we once put a chokehold on the game and cut off oxygen to the brain to make sure we were alone and there was no heir to head of the throne; like royalty with riches. But I will admit this, sometimes, this mad king just wanted to cause a sad scene by messing up your make-up, jerking you by wig, pulling you by your britches and yanking and hauling you by your ankles to show the true simple meaning of a drag queen. Then put my foot to your temple so you can really face defeat like a beat up kickboxing crack fiend.

And I know that seemed so blunt, but you can roll these words up for months and smoke my truth in a congested booth of sharp lies. Yet, you should never be scared or disguise the look in your eyes of being suspenseful. I will never look to violence for fear of the pen or really draw blood without a pencil as a syringe for a vaccine because writing is my only cure, and *my* antidote is not contagious. It won't save us or fix anything because we're already broken. You couldn't even cum back if I ejaculated on your spine and you were in doggy-style with legs wide open. That's why talk is so cheap, because that's all broke people can afford and will invest in, even when the words are congested and stolen.

Now I would never hold in my fears of you releasing a tear. Yet, even if I had to, I'd shout out my love for you to the world so they can hear. But, since you were my world, I'd just found it best to whisper it in your ear.

I just never knew I was here as chosen hopeful for my potential and possibility to be better, while I would choose you whether great or at your worst nerves. At that present time in the past, to my future, you were my gift, but now even my adjectives and nouns have actions to shift to hurt verbs. So, we're on this fuck this bitch shit, and somehow I became cursed words.

But, I still love you…for better or for worse.

For Momma

I was born the first thought of a good fuck purposely, not an incident or accident, but an instant significant infant from a little bit of nothing. Rested in my mother's belly for nine months and some change while she went through nine months of change and endured the pain and stomach rumbling of pushing and shoving innocence into a world of sin that has no mercy for the weak. And then I was expected to begin my life, and live it awake not sleep to become something.

And I've done that and I am still doing that. And it's all because of you. A single strong black woman raising a snotty-nosed, nappy-headed black boy to become the healthy, strong minded young black man you see before your eyes today. Together we took all the short cuts through hell from the project drug sells to kisses blown from jail cells in search of a heaven on earth with time to play and you were the only one that could have paved that way.

Making sure I wasn't led astray with your guidance and hugs. I was your last born; you were my first love. Shoved out, bare naked ass out into this world with little hands, you are my protective glove.

Catching any fast eight balls from crack fiends, you are the black queen that whether half mean, sad, or happy, you never hesitated for me, but made it snappy when it was time to pick up your other crown showing me how to be a king so you became daddy.

You were the jester when I needed laughs, the knight that saved my ass, and the servant that gave me nourishment in a glass and the food for thought. Yet you made me the prince of your throne and castle and taught me everything I ought to know about how life is sold and bought.

And though it always seems that we caught the shitty end of the stick you were still my rock and foundation. And you never forced me to go to church, even though your momma said you should cause it wouldn't hurt, it didn't matter because you were my savior and salvation.

You brought church home to me in your own personal way. You knew it wasn't about scriptures and dressing up on Sunday, but the message because the blessing is given in good faith on any good day.

Performing miracles on every holiday, it was like we used to have to save up to be broke. No lights, we lit candles. No cable, three channels. It even became a normal to bath in dishwashing liquid because sometimes we didn't have the money for soap so we thought our lives were in shambles.

But you never lost hope and were always there for us in ample time through all the joy and pain. Your blood runs rapid through my heart veins. You are the alpha and the omega. Even when the Atari broke, I got things I wanted instead of things I needed so you went out and bought the Sega.

Taught me to say fuck the haters because it's not what they think of you; it's what you think of yourself. I'm already strong with my right. Momma, you helped me to work on my left.

And I believe Pac said it best because there's no way I can pay you back. But my plan is to show you that I understand. Of all there bullshit we've been through, you are still my super Wonder Woman. And I've always tried to live up to be that son you could call your incredible He-Man.

I never sold dope. Never been in a gang. And sure, I was young, dumb, and full of cum so I may have stolen a few things back in the gap, but even that side of my life has changed.

Only your soothing voice can tame this wild flame and lay my soul to rest. And if you ever in life doubt yourself, though you never should, just remember I am your success.

And you are my trophy. And that's said with all the utmost respects. I just want to reassure you that you are very much appreciated and no words can ever be expressed. Because you're not only my rib, but also my heart it protects. Without everything about you, there'd be no me. So, I love you. Because you are the air that allows me to breathe.

From A Father

In the case of my unknown or untimely departure, I would like to leave my unborn son with these few words. To let him know I wasn't a victim of circumstance or some sperm donor, but I truly wanted to be there for his first words to be heard.

And to serve him with a message and lesson in life that my father never took the time out to learn me cause it's hard for a woman to teach a boy how to be a man. So when you fall, I want to be that dad that puts that band-aide on your hurt knee and old school you be the best man that you possibly can.

So just remember that any nigga with a dick can make a baby, but it takes a real man to be a father and take care of his child. It's okay to play the field for a while, just don't be a hoe out there and fuck every woman you see with a huge ass and a talented tongue behind a nice smile.

You should always have your own style because someday you don't want to be someone's baby daddy; you should be a father and teach this same lesson. If you don't, you could be stressing over some bitch messing with your money from a child support check, fucking with your credit, and missing out on all of life's little blessings.

So baby boy, just remember to learn from your mistakes. When greeting another man, always look him in his eyes and stand tall and always exhibit a good firm handshake.

And learn to never take a man for granted and control your temper and always keep your cool. I want to be there to teach my son how there's 12 inches in a ruler and how even in the summer 2 shirts keeps him cooler and protects him from peer pressure from the fools in the streets or the ones that may be in his own school.

Teaching him proper etiquette and attitude and the simple things like how his belt should always match his dress shoes. I want to be there. To be his father, protector, lawyer slash coach slash friend. I want to teach him to learn females' needs and be true to her so he'll never have to pretend.

Basically disciplining him into being a good man. One that doesn't think with the head between his legs, but the one between his ears. Sunday morning, I'm teaching him to tie a tie and taking him to church to be spiritual and that Jesus Christ, the Lord, and momma and daddy are the only folks in life to fear.

Wiping his tears as a baby, I'm going to pat him on his back to burp him and let him spit up on my shoulders. Sucking the snot out of his nose with a pump and putting a blanket on him when the weather gets colder.

Whipping out folder after folder of embarrassing pictures to family and friends showing his naked ass. That's my job. Those are the experiences I would never pass.

Because I would be proud of his lil ugly ashy booty black ass with everything that he doesn't do and does. And never in life be like the neglecting nigga and sperm donor that my father, and I know some of your fathers, always was.

Cause he will carry my legacy, as my times grow colder. Just remember the enemy of an enemy is believed to be a friend, but also just remember keep your friends close and your enemies closer.

You shouldn't have to look over your shoulder if you're a good man that respects others. But never let another brother take your kindness for weakness because you're big enough to walk away and become that lover.

Yet and still, it takes a fighter to be in love. I was born before him yet he comes before me so I would step in the eye of any danger and take that shove.

And being man enough to show my affections and give that necessary hug. Because he is a part of me and he should enjoy himself. I want to teach him to cook, clean, shave, and have a natural hustle in him to work to be independent and not need anyone's help.

So he can keep money in his own pocket. And shoot for his goals like a rocket that wouldn't stop if another found his accomplishment in a bubble and tried to pop it.

This is my message to my ungrown seed. If I'm not there for you, just know that I wanted to be there for you and your time of need.

I just want to be the father I never had. I want to be that dad that's in the stands making bets on his son scoring the next points or bringing the pain on the field from the three-point stance.

Making me relive my life through his. When he gets older and has children of his own, I'm going to be there to give a dollar to his kids.

Cause I'll do anything to stay in his life to see him make it and embrace him. Even if his mother and I were not getting along, I'd file child support on my got damn self to get that visitation.

Cause that's what a real man does. Not making excuses for himself because me and his mother are not getting along. Just know it will never be your fault if things between me and her go wrong.

Cause you are my life and I'd sacrifice my life for your life to be continued on living life. And I'd give it all up just to hold you in my arms one more time on any night.

So in the event that I don't get the chance to personally put these words in your ear. Just know I wasn't like some of these other sorry ass niggas that don't even care. I just want you to know that I do care and would give anything in life to be there.

One love from one father to one unborn son in one lifetime your life completes mine and I love you and you will always be number one to me in all of mankind.

So until we meet I will constantly wait for your existence. Just know that I love you with all of my soul and we will be together.

Ghost of The Ghetto

I want to tell you about the uncharted region of territory that I come from. A place that when the sun rises, it casts a gruesome a crucifying shadow of dissonance and even the chaos can weigh one ton.

In this jungle, survival of the fittest is a must with more emphasis on the bullshit so excuse me if I cuss. Just trust me when I say this is my story of the blind leading the blind so I will make myself an apparition of ghettos past and won't hush to put on your mind the good and some of my disgust.

I'm talking sexual exploitation within a white-owned black nation. I'm talking turning the little TV on top of the big one with grip pliers to the right UHF or VHF channel 39, 20, or 26 stations.

With dope fiends using the antenna for a pipe. With baby mommas making it fight night every night on section 8 and ain't trying to make their living right.

I want to take you to my home to a life on crutches where you have to work to be broke. Where nauseating smells from refineries make your throat choke or like dope fiends receiving cut up soap in good hopes that they're paying for good dope.

So I really want you to feel what I'm feeling. If I tell you it's cold there should be goose bumps on the back of your neck because the room is really chilling.

Witnessing the dealings with these hoes on the streets tricking they food stamps for treats that the dope man has been dealing. I'm the ghetto ghost of ghettos past so I want your shoulders to be saturated from a child's tears and feel his fear of a mother's death that may be nearing.

I want you to feel trapped behind the chipped and cracked bricks with no means of an escape. Living in a world where the good suffer and the bad prosper on any date.

Let me rape your mind and fondle your thoughts to fornicate your way of thinking. I'm living the reoccurring cycle of the lowest standard of living and I just can't get out because the blinding light of animosity keeps me blinking.

I just can't see my way out of this heated battle. It's like speaking into the cooling fan in the window; my words are distorted and shaken like the inside of a child's rattle.

I want you to wake up from nightmares in deep sweats and wonder what's next as bullets fly by the place your head rests. I want you to confess that your heart has beat out of your chest because some nigga has gained access to your home from fleeing from a crooked police officer's arrest.

Making your home his hideout in search of a refugee spot. The streetlights are like halos in the murk so why are your nappy head kids outside the church playing on the corner of the block?

Wasn't there just another shoot out the other day? Can you actually smell the stench of raid from battling with rats and roaches or the trash everywhere in the walkway?

In this life you're expected to fuck up. When you carry urine in a bottle to pass a piss test it's hard for you to luck up.

You have to learn how to live. That's the experience I want you to search for. Envision kids go up to the bootlegger's house for cool cups knocking on the doors with another nigga behind them asking for a four.

Or playing hide and go seek behind the dope house where the hustlers and gang bangers hang. Only to run into your friend's mother slanging her welfare check in hopes of getting a quick fix that hits her back like a boomerang.

Lying, thieving, inconsiderate, conniving, deceiving, freeloading, no business born, all of this is incorporated in the ghetto. Much depression, oppression, suppression, racism, poverty, drugs; violence stress and strain are just a few of the things I will never let go.

Men and women falling into the hands of temptation and becoming slain to the infamous name of crack cocaine. Some of the women are even pregnant but ain't a damn thing changed.

Making them deranged and pawning everything to hit that mighty pipe. I'm the ghost of ghettos past and this will be the last time I let this sad song be sung and let through on any night.

With a symphony of crying babies outside in diapers or spotlights from medics in helicopters to saving a man that was shot by the coppers makes this song a sad song of disappointment. Since I'm just an apparition or a figment of your imagination, there's nothing I can do to heal this pain by giving it some magical ointment.

I just want to have my point sent directly in between your temples. I'm the ghost of ghettos past and I hope I've made your understanding just at least a little bit more plain and simple.

Grandma's Hands

Imagine a pair of old hands. Shackled. Swollen and broken. Bloodied. Bruised and misused. Sweaty. Callused from malice. Healing. Withered and Blistered. From stepping in cotton fields to two stepping in the Cotton Club with Mister, nothing but wisdom and grace with each wrinkled palm to the face to kiss her, they added a generation of sensation even to a poor black kid's Christmas. Grandma's hands.

And they were heavy with burden with a light smell of Bourbon, but was able to fix and braid a switch when you were smelling your piss and cursing or being worrisome, then say, "hand me my purse, son, and get some candy," when mom wasn't looking. The rock and foundation. The soul and salvation. They molded high dollar dreams and washed cold collard greens, mustard greens, turnip greens, from chitterlings to snapping beans that were green, you know the deal, nothing compared to whatever full course meal of soul food she was cooking. Grandma's hands.

Soothing and cooling. Strong, yet brittle. Every wrinkled everlasting vein represented each single passing pain. They delivered and raised children from biggest to little and spoke in riddles to dwindle out life's hardships to protect you from the evils of the world. From listening to Sitting' on the Dock of the Bay to Slide, Miss Marry Met, Tweedle Leedle Lee, and Down Down Baby, Down by the Rollercoaster; no hands would be down to hold you closer, and even could snap a look, glaring mean, while she shook and clapped a tambourine with Mrs. Pearl every Sunday morning in church and worked overtime sweating out her curls, braiding hair with arthritis till they hurt and greasing scalps with the little girls giving life lessons about what's hidden under their skirts. Grandma's hands.

Only one to two manicures in her entire life. Or should I say man-to-cure. One husband…maybe two only if the first passed, so let me get it right. One exploited backhand could cut sight. What you sitting over there bragging that you got from your momma was alright, but this woman's hands made sure she could stand and had a chance at life. Made sure your future was bright, hand over your eyes, concealing strife, while others were left in the dead of night to fend and fight on their own, grandma's hands never left you alone. Grandma's hands.

Discolored, dry, and trembling. No mittens in the winter. No gloves in December. Swollen fingerprints of oppression to the forehead showed love to silence a temper and make you remember all that glitters ain't gold. Praying fingers interlocked like vines that rooted to her soul. Scripture preaching. Picture seeking. A figure creeping through the night holding an overcoat with one finger in the middle hole coming to suffer with you while you had a cold. Grandma's hands.

My mother's mother, just Salline Merchant's voice, alone, was punishment and rough. Taught me the difference between shackles and cuffs. The project's mother, Mrs. Myrtle Rice was known to be tougher than tough. And I know what you're thinking. Yeah, to you, that probably ain't much. But, even if they never do anything else for me, just like God, they have already done more than enough. The embrace. More than a touch. Her love. More than a must, above anything unjust. These old, beaten, bruised, swollen palms looked like they would harden, crust and then turn into dust. They showed and told a story of love, lust and trust that will never whither or rust. Grandma's hands.

Marlee

  Through one passionate shift in the night, I was able to give you the gift of life. But, you did me one better. In the grittiest of weather, you gave me the gift of fatherhood like no daughter could.

  Once deemed a slaughtered hood, you elevated me to higher heights to take flight farther and farther than a charter could. And even though my father stood in the absence of nothingness in the distant space of the wrong door, the only way I could be a good father to you was to give you exactly what I always longed for.

  I was able to be home more and more than excited to be there to receive the call, and to miss it, I would never take a chance of it. Because no matter how big, bad, and hard you think you really are, when a two year old hands you a toy phone out of a plastic car, you soften your voice and you answer it.

  So, please, excuse the French toilet, but I can no longer romance the shit and spoil it. I'm clogged and backed up and since I can't flush my system, I use the pain in my veins and whatever else is left within them to maintain since I can't drain them and boil it.

  So, when you're old enough, I can only pray that you're bold and tough to understand. You are the reason I've wanted to become a better man.

Pain and Sin

"Bitch, shut the hell up and just do what the fuck I say." Those words shocked the shit out of me too and always seem to ring in my ears. You see drugs rubbed daddy the wrong way so the loving hugs turned into tears from push and shove and added to my fears.

Reliving a life that was never lived and never was. They say the apple doesn't fall too far from the tree, so how do I know that apple didn't roll off in the mud?

Putting your hands on any female is one of the most cowardice acts. I don't give a fuck how much she bitches and moans, you have no right to react to that act and leave any scratch on her back.

I've seen the bruises, the busted lips, and the amount of tears that can run out of swollen eyes. Victimized by shackles of oppression, one of life's deep lessons to never have too much pride.

"But I love him." That's the type of shit I hear in between the scars and shattered glass that have led you down the wrong path. One of the seven deadly sins shows too often with him. You just won't acknowledge the anger fueling his heart when he releases his wrath.

You completely live in aftermath, so why do you constantly put up with this bullshit? No one envies this type of relationship. Far from love, being treated with total lack of respect in complete disgust. This motherfucker throws you against walls, cuts up your clothes and cusses you out and then has the audacity and greed to poison you with his hateful lust.

This is the worst monster seen in any child's eyes. And I've seen it. The back of a man's hands punishing the flesh of a mother's face. And then being forced away and to shut the fuck up and stay in a child's place. And I've dreamed it.

Sort of like watching a live cartoon take place before my very eyes. Photographic images of me screaming get your hands off my momma, and then being pushed aside in a fury disregarding all my loud cries.

This nigga is still getting high, so now what the fuck is a restraining order gonna do? Police can't be around all day everyday in this place. I remember the story my momma once told me of my aunt, when she was finally through with her man, he filled a coke bottle with chemical lye and dashed it in her face.

"Bitch, if I can't have you no one will," and now she's scarred and scorned for life. Poor woman's life ain't never been right. I even remember when my sister was taken against her right at the stroke of midnight and was threatened by a sorry mutherfucker with a gun. Pointing it to his own head. "If I can't have you I refuse to live another night." Just adding to her strife.

So I ask you, what's the justice for that night as the days grow colder? There is none, the flesh of skin on my collar has wrinkles from pouring tears that were cried in singles on my shoulders.

I just don't know what to say. If you really loved her you would just cool off the heat while walking away. Too much pain and too much sin can break down even the strongest men on any day. Maybe we all should just kneel down on one knee and look up to the Lord with these women in mind and just put our hands together and pray.

I hope you never have this story to tell on any night. This is dedicated to most of the women in my family that have had to put up with this type of bullshit throughout the course of their life.

And if any of you have ever had to go or are now going though this type of bullshit. Just get in touch with Ol" Skool, and I'll sure enough mob on him and slap that bitch.

Sunday Morning

I'm just waking up yawning
At the crack of dawn Sunday morning
To momma humming a new tune
That sounds like the church house blues.
Good smells coming out of the kitchen
Big momma just put her foot in it,
Yams, collard greens and spinach
And waiting for the final course to finish.
Tasting this and tasting that
And cutting up these and those,
With nappy head kids outside from playing with that water hose.
Momma say look at that runny nose,
Here grab a tissue and blow,
But don't sneeze and choke.
And you just woke up,
Go wipe your face,
Your eyes are full of crust and look kind of gross.
Now I got to do momma a favor and go to the store
And get some cranberry sauce.
She says stop tracking dirt in and out of my got damn house.
And you better not let them street lights catch ya
If they do that switch or extension cord gon' wrap and snatch ya
Up and I'mma skin you.
So don't pretend you can't hear me
Better yet get off that damn phone before I make you fear me.
She says she brought me in this world
And can take my ass out.
Then she told me to get my ass in here
And turn the TV station and watch my mouth
Before she got hostile.
I got to hear the good word, she says
And ain't about to be waitin'
To hear some of that good Bobby Jones Gospel.
That man's colossal words inspire and uplift
And have the gift of giving.
And after that I have to shift to my room
And don't come out till I clean it

Because she say it ain't suitable for living.
I hope she's not hearing
Me when I say she tripping
But I do it anyway.
Like when I shut up and stay in a child's place
Because I know she'll slap me in the face
If I don't obey.
She my momma and I know one day
I'll have to leave,
Not today, but one day,
So I cherish her even more in the morning every Sunday.

Temper Tantrum

After I woke up from this nightmare, I realized, in the darkness, that it was just a light scare, but I still peed in the bed last night. My daddy said it's not the dark that I'm afraid of, it's what may be in it. And although my daddy held me tight and said it was alright at that very minute, I still felt ashamed because I thought I knew better and should have done better.

I know I can only read one letter at a time, and when I fall and scrape my knee, my daddy's kiss can't stop it when it bleeds, yet still makes it feel great, fine, but I need to know what's going on around me this time, so tell me some news. I know I'm only two and I still love Dora the Explorer, Yo Gabba Gabba, and Looney Tunes, but I'll be three in June. So please try to explain to me the blues.

This is that awkward moment where I shouldn't be punished for acting just like you. I shouldn't have to go to my room or outside to play when tempers get to flaring and separation may just be one argument away, because if outside is so alive and great, why has man spent so much time trying to perfect what's inside to this date?

I don't care about who let the dogs out or why no one has ever found the way to Sesame Street. I'd rather know why gossip, rumors, lies, and deceit can stretch and run halfway around the world while the truth is still putting Stride Right shoes on its feet.

I used to wonder every week why dish washing liquid is made with real lemons while lemon juice is made with artificial flavor. But my daddy told me that whenever life gives you lemons, forget lemonade, make grape juice or chocolate milk then sit back and let the haters wonder how you did it from now until later.

He said whoever is trying to bring you down is already beneath you, never greater, and that though you may not be the girl every man wants, make sure you're not the girl every man has had for their own personal sinning behavior.

He said, accept your Lord and Savior because nothing changes until you change and everything changes once you change. They took prayer out of schools, but give bibles in prison, so my daddy makes me pray each and every night, in hopes that if I do it now, I won't end up in there later, and so my sins will be forgiven.

I used to sit there grinning and wonder why you never hear about psychics winning the lottery. But, now I only wonder why everyone claims they want, deserve, or even demand respect, yet fail to treat each other properly.

I love that I'm sort of my daddy's property. He told me to attract what you expect, and reflect what you desire. And to become what you respect and mirror the things you admire.

Instead of throwing me into the fire, he helps me be the best that I can be, even when tired, because he knows I can only read one letter at a time. And my daddy's kiss still makes whatever's hurting feel just great, fine, but I need to know what's going on around me this time, so tell me some news. I know I'm only two and I still love Dora, Yo Gabba Gabba, and Looney Tunes, but I'll be three in June. So please try to explain to me the blues.

I know when I cough, I may have the flu, but what boggles my mind sometimes is why they still sterilize needles for lethal injections. My daddy once popped me so hard for going into the street, I cried. I guess I'll have to turn five before I realize why he said that was for my protection.

His voice is my correction. I could care less how blue and yellow makes green. My daddy is why my pride is seen. My daddy gave up his wants, desires and a few needs just so I can dream.

He said that all men can change, and eventually all men will. But there is only one woman a man will change for so until he meets her, everyone woman gets exactly what that man can offer or give.

Ever since I was in a crib, many times I've seen my daddy cry. What he couldn't do or give, I've seen my daddy try. Santa Claus, the Easter Bunny, and the Tooth Fairy are not real. I get the gifts that my daddy buys. Sometimes he has to protect the way I feel. That's why my daddy lies. And, I know, if he had to, just for me, that he would kill. And my mommy will always be his alibi.

I just wish Tweety or the roadrunner would give me something from Acme so I could pry open my daddy's heart and take away the pain. On magical nights, I've even seen a waterfall from my daddy's eye while there was no rain.

But, you should never have to feel ashamed, daddy, I know you do what you can. I know that you can't be in two places, daddy, I know that you're only one man.

Just hold my hand, daddy. Pick me up and let's spin and twirl. I love it when I'm sitting on your shoulders. You are my everything, daddy. That means I'm on top of my world.

I can only be daddy's little girl because you are the only example of a good man that I know. Never a neglecting, mistreating, sperm donor or some drunken wino. My daddy's hardworking back is my pony. I don't care about unicorns. They're just phony. To me, unicorns are all just tall skinny anorexic rhinos.

Even when I go to Pre-school, I don't care if Ol' Skool can't buy Play School because he's always made sure I'm street-schooled, and clothed and fed with a roof over my head even when the bank balance is less than zero. A caped crusader with a dirty towel tied around his neck with old drawers on, daddy, you are still the best superhero.

Every time that we go to the park, I love it as you join in as I play. And though I don't believe you should get praise or props, or chocolate chip cookies or watermelon Lolli pops for doing what you should do as a man to stay, I give you my last scoop of strawberry ice cream with sprinkles on it, anyway.

Daddy, it's easy to judge the mistakes of others. It's hard to recognize your own. Daddy, it's easy to make mistakes. It's hard to learn from them, even when you thought it was already known. Daddy, it's easy to say I love you. It's hard for it to everyday be shown. Daddy, it's easy to hurt someone who loves you. It's hard to heal the wound when it's already to the bone. You can't always change the people that are around you, but you can always change the people that are around you or be left alone.

Daddy, daddy, someone please call my daddy. Get him on the phone so I can facetime. Without him, I have no identity and an unfulfilled, unshaped mind, and he can show you better than I can tell you or any friend of me about a good father with a great spine, so don't bother me about the reasons I don't hate mine.

That's why so many other little girls are lost through the grapevine, can't walk a straight line, falling victim to social hate crimes and men's cake lines with jail bait rhymes because their daddy's mental state's blind, playing peek-a-boo, and he never knew they could only read one letter at a time and only his kiss makes whatever's hurting feel just great, fine, and he would probably rather just chase dimes and pennies than take nine minutes to tell them what was going on around them so they shined, or wouldn't even give them a late sign in the daytime after playtime, making sure they find out the news.

And, H. E. double hockey stick, four letter curse word, no, you cannot take mine because my daddy is a one of a kind thoroughbred that I rate prime, that's winning this race I'm giving, and knows that I'm just two and I love Dora the Explorer, Yo Gabba Gabba, Team Umizoomi, Bubble Guppies, and sometimes Spongebob Squarepants, Blue's Clues, and Looney Tunes, and that I will be three in June. My daddy tries to explain to me the blues.

Even when I have a grown temper tantrum, he knows I get it from him and he is still there with a grin, walking proudly to his own simple anthem. You know him as the savvy, young cool dude they call Ol' Skool, but I gladly call him daddy, and for everything, from sad to happy, I just want to thank you…for just being you.

So, if you love your daddy the way I love my daddy, stand up and give him a hand, because I guarantee he fought more in the darkness than monsters under the bed and the Boogieman, just to be there and hold your hand.

True Story

She was only eleven years old. Her eyes were cried swollen and she was grieving. Victimized by a predator of her time. She was tormented, raped and then beaten.

Even when sleeping or day dreaming she could see flashes of the past evil. And to add to the pain she was taunted and teased by laughing people even more after being injected by the last needle.

And I'm not talking about the last measles, mumps and rubella's shot. I'm talking about something that has to keep her stable. Now, she had dreams of having children one day, but now I don't think she will even be able.

Her insides were bruised badly enough and along with her innocence they may have been crushed. And for a while afterward, she was like a silenced mute... speaking in a deafening hush.

Her eyes are flushed dry from tattooed tears and any thought of being touched brings back past feelings and a statue of fears. She hears voices at night. Is overcome by fright. And is cautious of any man that nears.

She's even been made fun of by insensitive peers that act like it's a joke. She lives a life in her own mind because she believes the outside world is broke.

For her, all good times were choked out of her and this is hell on earth. No one understands her and can empathize with her. And because of this she wishes she could reverse her own birth.

Life just isn't worth living anymore in her own troubled mind. An evil spirit rests upon her shoulders and seems to be on the grind, working double time.

And she comes and opens up to me as if we were at a confessional. What can I possibly tell her? I thought to myself. I'm no where near a professional.

All I could do was listen. Try to remind her that life is still worth living and if she was gone, everyone would be sad and really miss her. I even got pissed off more for her because it hurt even deeper as I thought to myself that this little girl could have easily been a little sister.

There are some sorry motherfuckers in this world. How can someone go out and rape anyone......especially a little girl.

Brainstorming

I need you to sit, don't speak and just listen. I must have thoughts missing because I can't remember any of the last times we've said we loved one another? I sense resentment. I'm in love, yet I get no love so could it be the secret visions of another lover?

For some reason it seems as if our love just slipped through a noose and committed its own suicide. Or like a bittersweet rose left dead in the cold on a winter night, it just fell, withered away and died.

Now I've cried out all the tears I'm prepared to lose over one woman, but with each passing moment, I find myself contemplating and rethinking about the love we could not keep. Asking myself why there were no sudden leaps to reach and seek that point and moment in life that everyone seeks.

This is the only time I've ever felt lonely in a relationship, so I wonder how did our lives come to this? We sleep back to back in bed, there are walls built up around us, and everything seems to be reversing itself ending with the first kiss.

I've tried to give my all, but it seems as if you don't want to even take the risk because you let the actions of a past love dictate your actions toward me. It's better to have loved and lost than to have never loved at all, but you have to get over that love because the walls you put up make me left out to be the enemy.

We're together, yet distant. Barely speak, but will argue in an instant. And when that love has been recaptured and found, it's lost with resentment.

So now who's to blame? It seems like the both us just have too much pride to even apologize first. Maybe from the beginning there was no real hunger or thirst for love and was like a timed bubble preconfigured to expand and burst.

I don't know but maybe it was cursed. But I do remember a time when our lives were lived sort of like a fairy tale. We used to overlook our own problems for each other's and were like distant lovers trying to unveil and live the type of love that would never sour or stale.

But I guess now that's in the past. I often find myself miserable to make you happy, yet every time I'm happy it seems as if you're miserable and have been bitten in the ass.

So this is my last confession. Us being together is longer going to happen. You used to be my rib in life, but now that rib is only for my heart's protection.

Dear Departed

Sometimes I wonder how it feels to have the sight stolen away from your eyes. To know there will be too many heartbroken tears and unheard good-byes.

The one who has passed and is loved most should and must always despise all of the lying cries in disguise.

And as you're pushed between the two worlds of darkness and light, there should be no worry cause to the place you're going you'll never have fright.

Something just doesn't feel right as my tears harden the softest ashes of my love for you in my heart. Maybe it's the striking blow and realization to me that you're gone, but my love for my lost one will never part.

Two lifetimes full of cherished memories. Your death, as the great Shakespeare used to write, was a treasured tragedy.

And I hope you're up there looking down on me, know that you've never been taken away from me. Every night I lay me down to sleep it is your face that I always see.

I paid my last respects as your casket closed and on top I placed a single long stem rose. And til this day, why I did this, no one knows, but it was for that river of love and respect I have for you that forever flows.

And since death is the only way the good Lord finishes what He started, this poem was written for you, the dear departed.

Forgive me...

    Please read what I have to say and don't ball up and throw away this paper. At least think about what I'm saying...and please give me some sort of response when you have some time a little later.
    I don't want you to stop being angry with me because you have every reason and right to be. I'm angry with myself because I hurt your heart...and I really don't have a full proof deniability.
    I'm not asking you to forget what I've done, cause that won't happen anyway. Forgiveness in due time is the only thing I can really ask of you for this day.
    Baby, I'm not trying to play games or live the lifestyle of someone I'm not. I truly love you, girl...it's when there's a chance of losing someone when you really realize what you've got.
    And I don't want to lose you, baby. I'd rather be with you even if you hate me. I don't want you to rush your decision now, just don't say no, at least say maybe. The thought of not being with you is driving me crazy.
    Maybe this small separation can clear what's hazy and bring us closer together. Being without you is like standing alone in the middle of a field with no shelter in the worst weather.
    We've been through too much together to let something like this tear us apart. And I know there have been times you've doubted my love...but the way I act when I'm with you should prove what's truly in my heart.
    Every aspect of you makes me want to be a better man. I don't want you to leave me, baby...and to keep you I will do everything and anything in my power that I can.
    So please try to dig deep in your heart because I know we can work this out. The tears I shed every night without you is drowning me out...because I love you without a doubt.
    Forgive me, baby, for I have sinned. I feel as if I'm losing a battle of a war that I know I can win. Please, baby...all I ask for is you to give me a second chance to prove my love again.

                    Forever Yours...
                        <u>The One You love.</u>

Gypsy Eyes

I want you to listen hard with your undivided attention because this is what it all comes down to. From time to time I often find myself in deep thought and meditation thinking about how you sometimes doubt the sincerity of a lover's love. Wondering if she's out there out and about giving up her bodily glove to another brother's love, inconspicuously betraying my love with her love of another brother.

Hopefully soon I will discover if I should further follow my suspicions and inadequate decisions to seek the truth, even though I know the truth might be something I don't want to hear, so why should I even bother? If I smothered this hypothetical situation with the theoretical temptations of the contemplation of her in the arms of another brother, should I indulge myself into a battle of wits knowing I could definitely find out about a secret lover undercover?

I really don't know what to say. I'm at a loss for words. Just thinking of another brother's hands cruising the contours of her curves is a thought that encloses me in my own cellular cubical of nerves in a sedated and comatose state. Not knowing if the love they make is indeed fictitious, and that thought enrages in me a ritualistic and transparent hate.

Raping me of the multiplying fallacies of true love and insufficient vagrancies of push and shove making it hard to act in a civilized civilian manor in an uncivilized civilian situation. Keeping my mind racing and heart constantly pacing making my visual and typical faces contort and distort from my mental visualization of their typical tantalizing lovemaking vibrations and deep felt sensations.

The eyes are the gateway to the soul is what I've always been told. I just can't tell how the whole mold of your soul unfolds, if it's like cold coals of ice growing from colder to froze or priceless like old gold stowed away at night or a pyrite mold, what the old folks' tall tales call fool's gold.

Seeing if your pupils dilate and tell the tale that beholds truth and can restoreth my soul and anoint my head in salvation of knowing you loved me. But like gypsy eyes, you've disguised the size of pride with deceit with lying cries of conniving cheat and instead of condoning me you surprised and shoved me. Cast out and ostracized me.

Befriended and then sinned me. The enemy of my enemy is believed to be a friend only this time he is also an enemy. Although I treated you with infamy, you just couldn't stay true to me.

You laid me down like a rug and treaded mud on me opening an irreversible wound with blood particles of disappointment oozing from the cuts with your sinful lust. Can you see the pain you've caused? Or are you too busy with the other brother to notice me holding my gut with him holding your butt while I lay in total disgust from the complete mistrust?

But you can trust my eyes won't shed but one tear from one eye duct. One tear from one eye of one man that symbolizes the one fear from one love lost that you just fucked so now you're shit out of luck.

I don't mean to cuss or mean to fuss for that matter. I just hope you realize what you gave up and it eats away at you like the malignant cells of cancer and the agony grows slows while you get even sicker and sicker and your emotions grow from sad to even sadder. You sorry ass bitch.

Never

Why'd I let you love me
You should have just been a friend
Outweighed the promise that you'd stay
When the love first began

I wanted you truly
Could have left my heart closed
Sent me in countless circles
Like revolving doors

Pulling me to the core
Like an emotional tug-of-war

See I wasn't yours
Heard that she wasn't either
Putting poison in me
As I tasted your ether

Long fits of the fever
Soaked and sweated your name
Bringing heat to my days
Left me cool when you came

And its hard to refrain
from a feeling so deep
all those nights with no sleep
cuz my body was weak

for the kisses and touch
that were never enough
so I drowned in the lust

he would thrust and adjust
to my bodily movement

as if I was the teacher
and he'd be the student

we would do this slow tango
to convince me that he was
the sweet answer to prayers

leave me layered in sheets
unable to speak

On My Mind

Now that we're apart, I really don't know what to do or how to act when I'm around you. We parted on good terms, so does that mean there's a chance of me being back with you?

Should I just forget all of the feelings I have for you and just move on? How do I know it's completely over and you won't change your mind when I'm gone?

I don't even know if I should I try to find someone else to love. It's just to too hard for me to start over. I feel empty every time I go out to a club and so complete as you get closer.

That's not something I want to do. I can't see myself out there back on the hunt pursuing different women to see which one comes the closest to measuring up to you.

Is it possible to love two women? I think so. Love is a man-made word and since man is imperfect, love has to have flaws and there has to be enough to love both.

Maybe it's best that I just go on about my business. And forget about all of the gentle kisses shared and jump back out into the game of cat and mouse and just risk it.

I should just find me another woman. You will forever be in my heart, but I can't wait and suffer myself in memories of you. I have to keep my life flowing on and running.

As much as it hurts me to do so, it's a decision I have to live with. I feel as if I would be cheating myself if I chain myself to the past and dwell on a life that's just become a myth.

I refuse to put myself through some shit like that. It's not fair to me to try and wait and put myself through misery waiting on a love that I'm not sure is coming back.

Maybe we are both to blame for what happened between us. Miscommunication, no consideration, just a bunch of bullshit that's left me in complete disgust.

So I guess this is my final farewell. I just hope life brings you happiness and whoever you end up with treats you just as well as I tried to.

Saying Goodbye

Baby. Listen to me. I have something to tell you and really don't know how to tell you this. You see... I've been seeing someone else, receiving their love from their own affectionate kiss.

Now I know this maybe seems sudden, but I've felt this way for some time. I don't want to hurt you, but I want to see if this second love has the capacity to shine.

You don't know this other person and I don't think the two of you should meet each other. I just don't think it's such a good idea for one love to meet a secret lover.

I don't want you to think this is out of the blue because I put a lot of thought into this decision. I've contemplated on all the pros and cons and something tells me I should follow the new vision.

I'm sorry for having to come to you in this manner, but I don't want to live this lie. I don't want us to be together, but I also don't want our friendship to die.

The reason I'm telling you this is because I care and respect you and I want to be a man about it. I don't want to play mind games or try to be a player or any of that shit.

I just want to tell you the truth and get all this off my chest. And for that I hope I can gain your respect and you'll give me your best. Goodbye.

Thank You

I was once told that I would become a better writer when I experience the greatest sorrow. So, who should be the person I thank for the way I feel now, today, tomorrow?

Conflicted. That's the best word I can think of that describes the way I feel. Confusion, sad, mad, disgust; all and all, a feeling that's totally unreal.

I feel alone like the smallest fish in the largest ocean with an absence of color or light. Like a dying soldier lost and forgotten on a battlefield in the darkest of nights.

So I ask myself why I feel this way. And even I don't know the answer. But this feeling is overriding my mind and eating away at my soul like the malignant cells of an incurable cancer.

The way I feel right now uses all of the saddest definitions of melancholy. The only way I think I can reverse this feeling is to have love, joy and laughter with the presence of another body.

But, now I have nothing further to say, so I guess I'm through. Oh, one more thing, I'm a better writer now, so I guess I should thank you.

Unfinished Business

Excuse me miss, but I'm a little pissed. It's come to my acknowledgment that we have a few semi-malicious things unfinished to discuss. It's nothing really serious, just a small list of unfinished business. You just can't just leave me like this to reminisce on the dizziness and punishment from the metamorphosis you insisted on taking before and after the last unpassionate kiss.

So why are you doing me like this? Baby, I know we have some undisclosed discussions and some unresolved issues. What did I do to deserve this treatment of cruel and unusual punishment? Why is it my feelings you're trying to misuse?

Why don't you give me a few clues and hints so I can better understand the situation at hand? I just can't stand being left in the dark like a man that's been ran and jailed to withstand the conditions similar to the conditions in the inside of a port-o-can.

That's just not me. I need to know what's really going on. I refuse to live my life like various notes of the blues, each track being another sad and confusing song.

There's just no justification for the wrong you've been treating me lately. If you hate me, tell me and don't rape me of the good life I've been making for myself, so just let me know if you don't want to take me.

Don't mistake me or try to play me for some ignorant fool that you can do away with at your willing. I've done you no wrong, but it's my heart and emotions that you're playing with and stealing.

Time is the only healing force that can make things better. I need to know whether I've been wasting my time with trying to be together with you or whether we can make it better and find a new way to never be apart again and just work on having a life of being together forever.

I would never do anything purposely to cause you hurt. Yet I feel you've just teased and flirted with my emotions like an expert then treated me like dirt after you worked overtime to tear a hole in my shirt to get at my heart and challenge its worth.

Is that the way it's going to be? I want you to tell me what you're going to do. I'm only cheating myself out of my own happiness if I try and sit here and just wait for you.

And that's something I just can't do. I refuse to allow that to happen and put myself in that place. So I guess this is my final farewell. The unfinished business we once had is now finished and closed but just know that your place in my heart will never be replaced. Good-bye.

Battle Ground

I have two published sex books which you say isn't the best look because you also say that sex poetry is for pussy poets and I don't believe this. This tells me you were probably felt on heavy wrong by Eddie Long and may be gay and like penis. Men are from Mars and you and another shameless man in Uranus has probably never been to Venus. So it's time for me to show you my genius since you've never seen this.

You're an out-casted peasant from the future, past and present that will forever be the last irrelevant sassy reverend with several homosexual medical-tested testicles playing freeze tag with three bad diseased fags with a cheap swag whose jeans sag and knees drag from moaning please dad while you smile and squeeze glad and ease sacks that seem sad on a scrotum rope down to the hot water in your throat…tea bags.

And I decree lad that on this concrete slab some can see that eager hunger like a flea mad on a beagle in the summer in my meager size. I could care less about illegal buys, gay peoples' cries or what evil lies within a steeple's guides.

I possess an eagle's eye in the regal skies, but you're nothing but a parakeet that's scared of me. There ain't no wearing me, you can't scare a G. You're just soft cream puff fake cupcakes…a Hostess named Sara Lee. You can't prepare for me, just beware of me. I'm what you barely see like a rare disease on a hairy p through a pair of jeans. And you're nothing but a ruthless, toothless canary flea on a dairy spree, trying to milk your thoughts out on your comfy couch with you, Shawshanks' Aryan three and other dudes, bare and free…puffing smoke up each other's asses… sharing weed. Apparently you need therapy.

But I'm airing three as soon as they pass the ball. Might even dunk on you with a mask and pause; shattering glass and all while showing my ass and draws. Not stopping till I crash and fall like a classroom brawl. And I will still be the first round draft-picking with my ass shitting in a bathroom stall without even going to a basketball casting call.

You see, my task is small, but my cost is great. I'm Tony the Tiger. You're just a Frosted Flake, or some soggy bait that's soft as cakes. So, whatever salt you shake on a sauced fillet, just halt and wait…because when the fog escapes it's an unlawful mistake to assault and hate,. I'm like the boss' great rawest steak on the edge of Rick Ross' plate.

I'll leave you lost in space, a coughing ape, while I chill on a hill on a coffee break and deal with your replacements while you waste cents on your date's rent. And I have no patience to make sense out of the tasteless, hate mess from your face dent because we're like a tsunami and a ripple in a lake's vent...on two different wavelengths. You know, you should have chrome bracelets with a spray on Elton John fragrance and be thrown and placed into a basement adjacent to a man with fake prints that still likes to chase dicks...or be raped senseless by Fleece Johnson, the booty warrior butt-naked on the pavement.

I know my fouls are flagrant but I won't tame this, I wrote this game shit. I know my dame thick. And that broke plain chick that you may be for sure claiming once grabbed my whole drained dick and still gave it that same cold Rick James lick. My unchained wit produces an insane spit that makes a lame prick's brain split...Kurt Cobain quit.

You should be on the Vegas main strip with RuPaul doing all with your Hanes slit wide open while you're in a three point stance being called Maxine for letting three big half mean black things penetrate the back of your defensive lines...call it bed raiders sack team. Such a sad scene. Get a vaccine. Some say that's really mean. And you got the swag seen of a drunken reverend drag queen that used to be a crack fiend pedophile molesting little oriental boys in black skinny jeans.

You homeless homosexual, you mad for real? You should be given a traffic bill under a bridge for a half a mil for holding up a rainbow bouquet of daffodils and a sign that reads 'Fag for Meals.' On this mic, I laugh and kill spitting these bullets like a magnum will. And any saliva that drips from my ironclad of steel parrot's bill is like an acid spill in a disaster film. Tormenting and raising havoc still...destroying these faggot hatas like alligators...Lake Placid kills.

Not even eight massive pills of Advil could stop your head from spinning and help resuscitate. My words alone would choke you speechless in the roughest way and gasping out of breath...suffocate. I love to hate. This is a cuss a gay, fuss and play, suffer day. And I must be great just because I'm thinking about granting you this gust of fate to strut away. Even on Mother's Day the brothers say that you're a lust mistake and a nut to waste eating bananas like a slut primate...probably fucking apes... licking juicy balls...sucking grapes... But, since you're only as tough as clay, I guess I'll just dust this gay punk bluejay off of the mic tonight...since I think that's enough today for this queer duck cliché.

Bitch's Advocate

I wrote this for the bitches. Now before I make a few enemies, I wasn't necessarily talking about women. Because some of you niggas are bitches, too. But right now I'm just talking about the bitches that don't know they're bitches, so I'm just going to give them bitches a couple of clues.

I wrote this for the bitches. For the bitches that dress to impress looking like a million bucks, but ain't worth a dime or a friendly fuck and go to the clubs broke free before whatever time and post up by the bar in hopes of a nigga buying her some wine. Let me come to you and offer you some shit instead of clearing your throat trying to throw hints when I pull my wallet out of my pocket to get me a drink and enjoy my shit. Bitch, buy me a drink. It ain't no crime. 'Cause this is 07 and I don't need no pick up lines.

But this is for them bitch ass niggas. For them bitch ass niggas that stink from cheap cologne with flash and front jewelry and rims still living with your momma at home and think when they buy a female a drink in the club, they got a girlfriend for the night. Get your small talk in and move your bitch ass to the right. You ain't got to follow her ass around the club trying to make yourself known. If she wants you, she'll find you, so stop cock blocking on the next nigga, trying to bump into her on every other song.

I wrote this for the bitches. For the bitches that would file child support on her baby daddy just because he dropped her sorry ass and left her mind in a wreck. Bitch please, and with all due respect, a child support check shouldn't be the direct retaliation of aggravation from one slick bitch to a slicker nigga 'cause his dick creeped, had and enigma and figured to dig deeper and sleep with a richer and slicker sista. File child support on that nigga if he's not a father to his child, not because you got your feelings hurt and he cramped your style.

But this is for them bitch ass niggas. For them bitch ass niggas that deserve to have child support on they ass and don't acknowledge they got a damn child 'til the end and beginning of the year for a dependent on your income tax. Worried about big cars and big rims. You sorry mother fuckers need to re-spend it and get your got damn priorities intact. If you took care of your child instead of worrying about them hood rats and handled your business during the year, you could consider it a reward for yourself if you decide to spend it for that.

I wrote this for the bitches. For the bitches that think they got the best grade USDA certified prime pussy meat between their legs in this motherfucker. Well, let me tell you something. Your shit ain't no different from nan bitch around here so don't think your shit go the hardest. Cause the fact of the matter is, if you worth the time, any nigga going to spread you wide and fuck you regardless. So your best bet is to make sure your head game is on point. Watch the Superhead video from beginning to end and end back to the start. Cause if you ain't giving head and another bitch is, don't be surprised if that nigga leaves you and breaks your motherfucking heart.

But this is for them bitch ass niggas. For them bitch ass niggas that walk around like they King Ding-a-ling in this bitch but can't fuck worth a shit and don't know they just around to pay the rent. For them niggas that can't tell that she just going through the motions with no enthusiasm, just huffing and puffing, faking orgasms just to make you feel better. And you think you smooth as leather. Cause if you ain't marinating that fish right, you just the main joke told at every female's gather around and get together.

I wrote this for the bitches. For the bitches that just insist on telling your best friend every got damn thing that goes on in your relationship. Curiosity killed the cat so if you tell her everything that's going on she might get a lil' curious to see if your man is really all that. And try to give up that pussy cat. Ain't shit we do in our relationship any of her fucking business. Cause you never know, the reason she keep talking down on him is to break y'all up cause her jealous ass may be secretly giving him ass and blowing him kisses.

But this is for them bitch ass niggas. For them bitch ass niggas that constantly go around lying on they dick. Knowing got damn well they ain't fuck shit. Telling your boys, "yeah I knocked that down," or "yeah I beat that up last week." Knowing got damn well you ain't even smelled the pussy meat. Nigga you too old for that shit cause your mouth is your own enemy. If you didn't run your mouth so got damn much, you never know, she might even want a fuck that's friendly.

So to all the bitches and bitch ass niggas that don't want to be bitches forever, you need to just get along. Just remember behind every real bitch is a bitch ass nigga that did her wrong and made her strong.

Bona-fied Beast

So, it's now been pen-scribed and certified. I've graduated and metamorphasized into a bona-fied mic ripping beast. Infinitely intricate with this syndicate of metaphoric lyrics to be my instrument of fight gripping peace to get into it when sensing it, and be an instant vindicate as I sin a bit with this pen to script my decadent signature on this mic ripping lease.

Willing to battle and recite until deceased, sort of like of like a beast battling a night slipping disease that tends to fight and feast like malignant cells of cancer. Wise men speak when they have something to say and insignificant ignorant fools speak just to say something so you can now ask me, what's the answer.

Known to be a microphone enhancer and sometimes a romancer as I put lame lyricists and punk poets to shame in this game when I reign and rain words of fame till the point they get sick quick and need an infinite stick of valium. Some of you probably couldn't give away two flash drives if you cut a double downloadable disc album.

But, let me break it down some. You're weaker than seven days. Probably a cheater with seven gays. And you can never be better than or even fresher than a known veteran with a letterman that's been a paid speaker of seven plays, charging no cheaper than seven pays, that can spit heat to burn and beat ya and feature in seven ways.

I'm like the grim reaper of seven plagues from seven sins and seven prays that can burn the sensor strip even with censorship as I let this pencil tip rip and flip as I spit subliminal delinquent shit through my dental strip from a mental clip. So, if you use your common sense you'll get to know that my utensil grip of the mic is gorilla, and nothing is goes realer than this suspenseful trip.

I slipped Chucky a nightmarish parental slip. Gave Hannibal Lecter a cannibal lecture on fruit nectar. Cracked Jason Voorhees over the head with two forties, hit Freddy Kruger with two Rugers, and use a match and raid and sprayed hot fires at Michael Myers. And it took seventeen muscles to smile, forty three to frown, but only four and some Prozac to reach back and bitch slap the Zodiac when he was being a liar.

Sucker MC's can now call me sire. And just as sure as I know a private partial pure pounded piece of Ms. Piggy's pretty pink pussy is perfect prime pork properly prepared on a purple plastic or paper plate that Peter Piper picked a peck of pickled pepper for Pam's panties to pimp and play Peter to pay Paul pennies for poppies, peaches, and pears to add on a papyrus list with no purified grapes, I know that patience, practice, perseverance, persistence, and proper prior preparation prevents piss poor performance on any preceding date.

I make father time impatient to wait as I ship mother earth's ass full of dirt to the moon. And I wouldn't care if you called me sambo, jiggaboo, spic, spade, jungle bunny, or a coon, but if you ever call this nigga lest than the best you can rest assured that I will be getting on that ass soon.

Because I'm a bonafied beast…unchained and off the leash. Spitting hot grits and grease through my teeth while high stepping in Nike spiked cleats like Spike Lee on haters and perpetrators that can't deal with this night's defeats.

I mean my style is so unorthodox, yet concrete, ignorance and impotence has never had any significance of remembrance in any instance of any verses. Anything lest than the best is in my world is just completely worthless. And some may use vulgar language and curses because they can't get better rhymes to surface, but me, shit, I use these motherfuckers because it's the best got damn way to get my fucking point across when it disperses.

Not even nine naughty nurses in nine funeral hearses could save you from the furious fluid flowing flow of words from my last breathe. Because the last drop of saliva that drips is like a drop of alcohol that can drip on a scorpion's back to make it go crazy and sting itself to death.

So, yes, as you can guess, bitch, this is it. It's no coincidence. My rhyme's a malignant epidemic that's meant to hit, and you've been sentenced for time in solitary detention in my mind's imprisonment. So, envision it and sniff a bit to see something different, and get a good whiff of it without being a misled innocent hypocrite that repents from it in a sense that you never figured my sensitive pandemic instruments of vindictiveness would be intricately infinite intense offensive shit with a definite twist in it, yet still have an evident degree of defense in it.

And, one consequence of it all is that I still get infinite laughs and kicks from it because I know lost you with that last sentence, since I'm sensing it, so I will now try to restate my thoughts without a lisp in it while condensing it…and take the thoughts of you out, which is the bitch in it just to say the least shit. And just reiterate that fist line of hell since I was sent from it, piece bit by piece bit, to let my hot grease spit just to remind your cheap, simplistic ignorant ass that I am a mutherfucking beast, bitch.

Crack Cocaine

I want everyone to try to follow my fast paced talk and game and let me introduce my name as the Infamous Crack Cocaine. Ask me again I'll tell you the same. I can never be tamed cuz I'm to blame in this insane world of pain, fame, and shame.

My slang name terms have no ending, money I been spending. Damn, I should have a patent pending cuz even in the beginning I been sending men and women to their pockets grinning knowing they're sinning and constantly thinning cuz this adrenaline rush I be giving is too genuine like sitting with heroine in them and I can't be disciplined like ten feminine women throwing a javelin and aspirin can't even stop the oxygen in your head from spinning in the wind.

And I'm always winning cause I can make you broke, throat choke, miss a note, skip soap, elope, or hang from a rope full of dope. Now make a note, I don't sugarcoat so don't misquote that quote I wrote and seal it in an envelope cuz you'll devote and give an oath to demote me and denote me but your vote is overwrote cuz there's no anecdote. I even brag and boast when you float outside the boat looking like a goat gazing at the world through my periscope, long telescope showboating seeing your life pass through my broken distorted, contorted kaleidoscope.

You'll show up and soak up, open up or close up, hoe up or blow up, barbeque or mildew, kill you or spill you, will you and drill you. I can be the most powerful man in your life cuz I add to strife when you grab my pipe or use that knife to cut me right on that small glass mirror, that's what I like.

Become a chef tonight; cook me, cut me, boil me, shake and bake me, make me, take me, fry me, date me, rape me, play me, sauté me, but don't displace or mistake me, I'm your best friend. Later you can hate me, try to shake, or escape me, but I'm here to win, so go on and commit that sin my friend and lets begin a new life and set a new trend.

Go on and spend your money honey. Buy my twenty, be the dummy, to me it's funny, now you're clumsy, looking hungry, you can't run me, you try to shun me, I can be a hard white horse or soft lil bunny. You can even gun me or hit and run me, everyone has done me, so come on honey be a flunky and run with me, you'll never leave me once you've begun me.

You don't have to sacrifice life to receive or please me. I just need your spare change. After a while you can steal things, go home and pawn things like diamond rings, or hit a stang and give them to the dope man so you can bounce like a sprang and feel the bang of that strange tang coming back at you like a boomerang. I'm that vampire's fang that rearranged your body to be like a mustang and changed you into that estranged deranged that like to sang with a short attention span with a short life range.

So come on, baby, make a change, I come with no contracts. I can have you in the night like a bat or scrounging like a rat trying to get that, hit that; women suck dick to get that, hit that; men lick splits to get that, hit that; can you dig that even when sick from that you can't rid that, omit that, or admit that I'm a misfit that makes you act like hypocrite jack that takes no slack in breaking hearts through the veins that will stab you in the back.

So go ahead, wrap your lips around my glass dick and take that, hit that shit with the blue flame with no shame and puff slowly so I can be inhaled into your brain.

Let me play a game with your mind and bend it through time with my riddles and rhymes so your unconscious mind in time will be mine and under my spell to make you rob. I'm the work that loses jobs, cheese that hood rats mob and rocks that can make an alley cat sob.

Whether your name is Jesus, Jose, June Bug, Ray Ray, Susie, Moesha, Johnny or Billy Bob don't worry there's enough of me to go around. Let me take you for a trip out on the town. Don't be a clown and put me down. I once was lost but now I'm found so drown your life in my smoke and mirror frown. I can be an ounce, a pound, a crumb found on the ground, or just hanging around hounding you with my sweet sound that surrounds a clown and leaves you dumbfounded, schizophrenic or paranoid bound when you wear my crown or ride my upside down astounding underground merry-go-round.

Pound for pound in my town, your town, uptown, downtown, H-town way up to Chi-town and all around, I am the greatest heavyweight in the ring. Because of my schemes, niggas have rings that glisten and gleam, shiny things, hoes that sing, more money that's green, and selling me makes dreams a reality like being king of a fling that can make the hardest nigga become the softest queen in a prison scene.

Here's a new theme. Do you believe women hide me in cocks, men in socks, or safes with locks? I come in powder or rocks or bricks off docks and often shock jocks, as the clock ticks and tocks cuz niggas pack glocks around heads that flock to get my mighty rock and will break locks to feel my electric shock.

In the words of the late great Tupac, all eyes on me. Love me, touch me, tease me, please me, feel me, hit me, just don't leave me or deceive me. I'm a master magician, can't you see. I speak with no lips, feel with no fingertips, grab you with no hands and can lead you to skip and turn flips or get naked and strip, or flip the script and make your pants unzip and make you hip to take a trip on a sinking battleship.

I have the power to leave you hypnotized and left dazed in a trance. Just come give me one kiss, baby. Let's have some love and romance. If it's not, I'll give you a second chance.

Don't believe all the things you hear about me. I've never fucked up a life completely. I've never given complications to an unborn baby. I'm spoken of in the worst way politically. I may be seeing your favorite celebrity. I'll never mess you up mentally, physically, or socially, and I've never made a crack head give birth in an alley.

So what's your worry, baby, what are you waiting for? It's time to get on the floor and score, I might be behind the first door and behind the second there may be more. Let me be the one you adore; I can be your favorite chore and make your mind soar if you explore me and store me in you with an encore for more and let me be the sole proprietor and contributor of that eager roar that comes even before you lower yourself to my powerful, swift and controlling sword.

You'll never become bored. The only set back is a little stress and strain. Like the rain that drains, one kiss from me relieves that pain. Let me be that missing link in that unbroken chain that maintains the strange pains and gains obtained in or to maintain a life that's only domain is a painted flame with cocaine that hangs in a drain soaked with rain. So come on and play my game. My name is the Infamous Crack Cocaine, ask me again and I'll tell you the same. Try me once and I guarantee you'll be back in the game with no shame.

Cut Throat

Now Jathod already said that these men tend to spend and gamble against the odds, and do not fear God or respect any of the unwritten laws...even if they pertain to us. But even I used to live my life unbalanced on a tripod; my middle name was dangerous.

And some hoes still wear stilettos 'til their ankles bust even after they've been beaten like other mangled sluts until their souls burn then turn to ash. And some will sniff it from an urn till they pass just because it is fallen angel dust.

And though at the time no one could untangle us I just have to admit...your lust was just some incredible shit. I mean it was on point like a decimal list, but, to be honest, I'm not known to relay a false promise. You were just another hoe.

You should keep bullshit thoughts close and never tell your next of kin the details of your quest to win. I knew you were trying to have me at major medical unable to flex again, but you see me...I'm also cut throat.

Known to fuck hope in a stuck boat and draw a severe tear in fear when near and kick a pup slow 'til its gut pokes from cracked bones and have other stuff broke as it suffocates and I huff and wait till that mutt chokes. Now just so you know... that was actually just another slut hoe.

I'm spitting lemon juice to razor blade inflicted wounds, adding insult to injury with a bruise. I know for a fact that some niggas will rape your carcass in a tomb.

I consume the soul of the reaper for a cheaper price of life because I also do not fear death. I'm afraid of that moment before the moment my heart lingers and shakes in my chest and fingers break as I hold on to my last breath.

Damn...That soon brought more tears to her eyes than before as her heels bore holes in the pavement. Too many souls and spirits have surfed on two different wave lengths ever since her wrists wore bracelets that Jake the Snake spent more than enough of his dollars and common raped sense of impatience.

But you just couldn't face it. A nigga will wear no glove, showing slow love, and leave fake prints of greatness. He will even leave home alone with no cologne and return with the flagrant stench of another woman's fragrance.

But, good men are not hard to find. You just can't chase a man that wants to be a bachelor. You may think he's spectacular with his vernacular, but he'll flip you like a spatula, drain you like Dracula while smacking you up against walls and not keep in contact with you while he's taxing you with a fraction of his flaws and lust.

    Baby girl, there is no need to fuss. You still are a foxy lady and I do mean very beautiful. I'm just cut throat and used to the bull. Just don't let this mental pharmaceutical cause you to get delusional to a point where I'm reading your tombstone's epitaph and the eulogy at your funeral.

Don't Judge Me

How can any motherfucker in this world try and judge me? You don't know me, you don't know what the fuck I've been through and seen, so how in the hell can you hold a grudge against me?

Why is it when you look at me all you see is my pigmented black skin, cornrows, and a doo-rag? Is it my physical that intimidates you, or is it from time to time when you see me, my slang is bad or pants may sag?

Does that shit make you feel insecure, upset or mad? Tell me what the fuck is on your mind. The way I look and rhyme ain't got shit to do with anything inside of my head and mind, which should make me blind to any ignorant fool of your kind.

So go ahead and tell me just what the fuck you think you know about me. All the gossip and shit you hear on the streets just adds to the rest of the stereotypical nonsense and bullshit that's already propped up against me.

Is it the fact that I come from the ghetto projects and have the capacity of having a thuggish mentality? I speak my mind occasionally and will do damn near anything for my family. I make my dreams a reality and do the same shit you do to try to better yourself in this corrupt ass, fucked up ass world we call the land of the free.

I tell you what; how about you sit there and listen so I can tell you the truth about a real nigga like me. First of all, my name is Howard McAfee, not boy, hey, or man. If you want my attention, it's mister, sir, or excuse me, you know the type of shit you say to respect any authority figure or any grown man.

I'm not a fucking child. So don't just say whatever pops up in your mind. And please don't try and patronize me and insult my motherfucking intelligence with the rest and best of your bullshit, tired lines.

I've heard that rhyme before and that entire razzle and dazzle; smoke and mirrors shit don't impress me. I tell you what; let me enlighten you into the mind of a motherfucker that you think is weak.

Have you ever had your ass beat to the point you can't speak, yet your mouth is wide open? Have you ever lived without lights or water or damn near froze in your bedroom as a young child because you had to tape a black plastic bag to a window that was shattered open?

I'm talking totally broke or been choking from nauseating smells that could make a weak stomach hurl, burn your nose hairs, or bring tears to your eyes. Do you know what it feels like to witness a nigga beat and split the head of a female over lies, on your porch falling into your living room, disregarding all of the screams and all of the deafening cries.

You know the meaning, but do you know the true feelings of suppression, oppression and depression, or any other word that incorporates a fucked up life? Do you know what it's like to have to see, touch, and speak to your mother behind a bulletproof, two-inch glass before night over some bullshit past or been chased for life by a cracked up motherfucker that has a six-inch blade knife?

Fuck naw, that's not you on any night but I've grown stronger because of this type of shit and all of my past struggles. And motherfuckers don't sympathize for me because of my past, present or any future troubles.

Even if they double, I don't want the satisfaction of you feeling sorry for me. You can't relate to any of this shit, so don't ridicule me and say you feel me or know where I'm coming from.

Shit, I ain't dumb. Don't let my grammar and word choice fool you. Some people call me "Ol' Skool", so don't get it twisted, motherfucker, I will school you.

My mind has the capacity to rule you and I will do you if you want to test my wrath. So, how, in the fuck, can you compare yourself to where I come from and where I've been if you've never been drug kicking and screaming down a similar path?

My people have been in and out of jail; I've lived through and prevailed from what some folks would call hell; I've had to open tons of mail from my mother just because she couldn't make bail. I've had to deal with a sperm donor who ain't worth a crack bitch's wicked and crooked spell in hell; I've even been trapped behind the chipped painted bricks and cold steel of a locked cell; You don't even know what it's like to have the jaws of life enclose on you like the inside of a clam's shell.

So motherfucker, don't you ever judge me or think I'm weak. Of all the bullshit I've been through my strength has no limits and I'm never afraid to open my mouth when I want to speak.

I've experienced depression, oppression, suppression, poverty, racism and all types of injustice. Shit, I come from a life of much unnecessary roughness.

Even the toughest niggas I've seen feel pain and shed tears. Don't take my kindness for weakness and don't you ever think the power of my wrath is nothing to fear.

So Motherfucker, just remember I am a stranger to you and you have no idea what I'm capable of doing. I might can steal the sight from viewing and snatch the teeth out the mouth from the chewing.

So if you don't know me don't ever hold a grudge against me. You better check my pedigree before you ever try and judge a mother fucker like me.

Don't Judge Me Again

This is to that hoe ass nigga that still wants to judge me. I thought I told you the first time, but apparently you still want to hold a grudge against me.

I usually don't repeat myself, but this time I'm glad to make an exception. I can see the hate in your eyes and I'm just flattered that I'm a key element in your perception.

Most all history is based upon deception, but me, I'mma give you the bone hard truth about me. I'd rather break you down with my words so you can go home and tell the youth about me.

Cause I know what it's like when it seems as if the roof is falling and you're stuck in a room with four walls and no window. When you've done everything right in your life and won every fight but still not the champion or the number one contender.

Nigga even in the winter I've had to deal with the weather with no sweater and no gloves for my blistering hands. I've been harassed by a white lawman just because I fit the profile of any other black man.

And I know it sounds like another sad story of a mad nigga on a bad rampage. But I've earned my stripes and my right to speak so I'm bout to unleash myself and my words like a wild animal from a steel-clad cage.

Nigga have you ever had to bathe in dishwashing liquid cause you couldn't afford soap? Or just lived any part of a life where it seemed as if you had to save up to be broke?

I've been poked in the side of the head by the barrel of a gun with a white policeman's finger itching on the trigger. I know I look like your average nigga, braids, dressy with gold, and a muscular figure, but don't you ever classify me as another drug dealer.

Even if I come from crumbs to bricks and rags to riches if you don't know my struggle don't judge me on any night. It takes the strongest to show weakness, so this time I'mma beat you with my words instead of starting the fight.

So don't you ever in life turn your fucking nose up at me! Shit, I was at my strongest even when I've had to cry myself to sleep; cuz I've watched my daddy creep; I've witnessed my sister beat; I've even had my feet in a puddle of blood that may have been an inch or two deep. I have painful distorted contorted childhood memories of me I'd even love to delete. I've even seen beat downs from nigga to nigga over many frivolous defeats, even if the nigga didn't even cheat.

So now what do you think of me? I wish a motherfucker would try to judge me. Some females love me and some may hate me, just remember some of your women want to date me. Some even say they will rape me and some probably won't take me, but I don't give a fuck, I'm a self-contained unit and can't nan hoe make me or break me.

So don't mistake me or take me for an ignorant nigga that don't shit about what he speaks about. Knowledge, common sense, and street awareness are just a few of the necessities I've never been without.

But I've been without a jacket in the rain. My mother's tears have saturated my shoulders with tears from pain. Yet, at times I've had no parent's shoulder to cry on when I've had it hard to maintain. Fuck, for a child, I've had too much stress and strain; a bunch of shit that would probably drive your kind insane, like the weight of the world crushing down on your brain.

Even in the rain, heat, and cold, 150 feet in the air holding a pole in a plastic suit on two feet of wood, I've worked every day outside in the motherfucking elements. 16 hours a day for weeks to months in a refinery while you thinking I sell weed in blunts and you trying to judge me is motherfucking the thanks I get?

Bitch please, I should be a reverend with this sermon I'm throwing to your brain. I'm a true blue-collar hustler, and I've earned everything I got through tears and sweat, disciplining myself to take the pain.

But I've never had shame or had remorse for any of the shit I've been through. I can withstand and take a lot of bullshit.... unlike you.

So the next time you ever try and judge a motherfucker like me, hold your tongue and thoughts in your head. You don't know shit about me, man. You can take the time out to get to know me or turn around and move your mother fucking legs, bitch.

Grand Slam

How in the hell did you ever build up the nerve to try battle and slam me. Everything you saying sound like the next man and I know I heard that shit before so nigga you a damn thief.

Trying to play me with your low vocab with your brain riding in a short special slow cab thinking you what it take to be a tough poet but just really a fucking fake. Nigga, I see I got to spit more venom in your ear to infect your thoughts and poison your brain just so you can see and feel how long my work takes.

My mission is to completely annihilate any competitors trying to compete in competition, so come step up and battle. I got enough strength and confidence in my tongue that I can use my teeth to and snatch rattle the horns off a whole got damn herd of cattle.

So I advise you not to even sit in the saddle because my flow is a shower of lemon juice and my words are the razor blades. Even when I write, you get a thousand paper cuts and the letters don't even smear when you holler and bleed under the shower when I make it rain.

I come to bring the pain and pity the fool like Clubber Lang when I decide to verbalize and metamorphosize into my alter ego the lyrical beast. Even if I had laryngitis and mumbled with a bad stutter and lisp with tonsillitis and I was tongue tied with cotton mouth and the hiccups on my worst day with a bad head ache, on any day I'd beat you even with an impediment in my speech,.

You could even add two busted lips and lock jaw to the list to see. The shit I spit is too raw like a man with halitosis and missing teeth so just know it, you could never fuck with me.

I'm that poet women love to see so you better duck and retreat when I spit fire because I refuse to be dethroned and stripped away from my empire by that bogus shit you spit like a hard liar. I'm a real poet, bitch. My verbs can make you sweat and perspire like you were a tired rape victim in a penitentiary for a cigarette hire looking at a barbed wire fence hoping you can get inspired to jump that shit.

Nigga, I'm that poetic vampire that retires dumb shit because the force of words that escape from behind the canines of my teeth bring pain and drains any rhythmical fluids and lyrical liquids out of any competitor's neck before it reaches their mouth. Making you choke, gag and cough just because I drained the sounds from your esophagus before the words reached your tonsils to slide down your tongue to slither out.

My gangster is what you're testing. I spit truth, nigga, no bullshit no deception. This is a battle of wits and I see you're unarmed, so I'd rather go home and look in the mirror changing clothes and battle my own reflection.

Or commit suicide by giving myself a lethal injection just so I'd forget I wrote this poem. I'd rather be my own reincarnation just so I'd have some decent competition when I'm reborn to battle my clone.

That way I can check out myself wreck the mic and see which looks better the waves, braids or a picked out afro. Better yet I'd rather be a spectator and sit next to you so I'd put two lights behind me and watch the next show of my silhouette battling my shadow.

You not even in this race. They could give you a Cadillac and me a turtle back and you'd still be in last place.

Because your words do not inspire, they have no meaning and do not uplift. Like my mentor said, my style ain't no hobby, son my style is my gift.

And the great gift of gab to get you going is what I'm gradually giving you. As a matter of fact, you should just take the mic home and let it live with you and use it for a sex toy cause I can already see the bitch in you.

I am not just a youngster spitting for fun, I'm trying to get my chips and the dip with a pencil. I'm the Loch ness monster spitting from a manuscript holding the mic with a panther grip as my eating utensil.

So I hope it's not too suspenseful when I say I'm eating these pussy poets with the flick of my tongue. You get satisfied by fingering the mic thinking you done won, but me, I never settle for less cause I'm so cold blooded I make the microphone nut up, shiver and cum.

I Ain't Welcome

Tell me just what the fuck you mean I ain't welcome here no more. Just because I move out this bitch and made a better life for myself how you gone shut the doors to this motherfucker, and say I'm not welcome in the ghetto.

You need to let me know something cause I ain't for this bullshit. You can miss me with that. I come from the same shit you been through and to the hood I aint never turned my back.

I know about cereal and water, syrup sandwiches, peanut butter no jelly or no loaf of bread to make that sandwich with. But now I ride peanut butter buck hide with jelly paint outside with deep-dish lips and am making that bread and butter and is still stacking my chips.

You can't bullshit the bull-shitter cause this ain't my first rodeo. I don't need the flashy lights, fans or a commentator, I done been on the bull before.

So don't come at me with this bullshit cause you will never be a better man than me and win this race. They can give you a Cadillac and me a turtle back and you'd still be in last place.

You can take a nigga out the hood but you'll never take the hood out of me. Old fools, convicts, and ex-tricks raised me and they were the ones that made me proud to be.

So how in the hell can you try and revoke my ghetto pass? Bitch, I'm gone let it do what it do regardless so you can kiss my naked black ass.

I'm a living legend in these streets and nigga you will never take my crown. I done did too much for my entire community, so how in the fuck can you say I ain't down?

Man I could drown you with my involvement and the respect I get in the hood. The riddle of life stumbled over the riddle in me and I was destined to be an inspiration when I was still up to no good.

Nigga you need to be like me cause I've never been a follower, I've always been a leader. I've volunteered my community service hauling material and laying sod in the blazing hot sun like a Mississippi slave for the preacher.

Turning non-believers into believers. Showing my love for my corner, my block, my set, my hood, and more, after I moved out before the not so good event of nine eleven. The social fraternity group I used to step in was one of the main reasons Texas City was that All-American City in 1997.

Nigga you used to come see me perform onstage and hoop and tell folks that's my nigga back in the day when I did all the things that were done. Me and my niggas even got together in 2001 and helped the flood victims in Houston from hurricane Allison.

Motherfucker, I've raised money for various charities and events. And niggas never tested me in the hood cause they knew I was never afraid to raise my hand and slap a bitch.

My street credibility is high and I will remain amongst the top players. You just a known felon in the hood but I'm respected well and has never laid down to any of you haters.

Yeah, I moved out, but that was just to get away from the nonsense from some of these fools. Bitch, I ain't welcome. Motherfucker, I used to tutor some of your friends and even help your dumb ass in school.

Nigga I've worked too hard for all the shit that I got. I chose the right path for me. Man, I don't need to hustle on the block.

And because of that all I do is fuck with top-notch bitches. I've had dollars worth of dimes in the stable and nigga you'll never see these riches.

Don't get me wrong I will mention the things you've probably done for me in the past, so I guess I can thank you. We used to be the thugged-out boys in the hood, but now nigga you need to respect my motherfucking gangster.

I aint no prankster no more. I'm on my grown man shit. I'm about making this paper and nigga you need to get out and get your own got-damn shit.

Telling me I'm not welcome in my hood, nigga you stuck here and I got an open invite and that's plain to see. Bitch I am the hood, and nigga you ain't nothing but an infectious parasite, and bitch you and whoever thinks the same on any night aint ever welcome in the hood to me.

Kryptonite

Go ahead and put him on Death Row because I feel like singing. So, I guess you can call this as a Shug night, but his pride will only be "The Color Purple" once I climb on top and do my business to work him right with these words I'm laying.

This is lethal injection to the lungs of a man that never should have survived a lot in jail. You're better off greasing your hand and playing with yourself than rather gasp and waste the inhalation of your last breath, because if you think you can beat me, you're better off putting a syringe neatly to impale a demon's veins or a pistol up Satan's nose to blow out his brains because that's the only way you would have a shot inhale (in hell).

And before you breathe, look, it's time to get this cheese, so normally I'd say lettuce all grind all this beef up together and come up out of our shells like taco dinners. You and your squad, I got them figured. Your whole team is just a soft circle of squares…waffle niggers.

And I didn't become one of the hottest spitters by writing bullshit for applause, praise or laughter, too. While you may keep the people thinking that when it comes to slams, you are the last to lose, here I am making the bed rock like Bam Bam; known to act a fool. I'm desired like parents wanting healthy kids that have to choose the next free-of-charge iphone leak…apple juice.

My words are like those a pastor uses, that's a gift, known to uplift, save the suffering and soothe the hurt and sickened. You would probably just quote the bible and change your religion to Muslim for protection of the worst in prison. You're better off having a religious sacrifice of a pork chop sandwich with a white woman at Church's Chicken.

So as the plot and the verses thicken, you probably just think that I'm just trying to come back out and make a name for myself, but that's really not the case. I'm just trying to make them forget *your* name and face like a slave owner that caught you fishing with no meat on the line, and wouldn't let you off the hook so he made you whip with yourself…masturbate (master bait).

I'm cold enough to make your girl ask to wait to take off my belt to smack her own ass curves and enter my log in her world wide web every time we pass words. I'm among the elite of certified legends…and even if I divide that last word, she still wouldn't know where my third leg ends when I bend her over back words.

I could really care less like Casper, if I'm getting on your last nerves. I'm like a drugged surgeon on an operating table when I slang this lyrical crack...a dope doctor. And you're about to lose your one life to live, I'll put you in a general hospital within the hour and have your girl singing high notes after slurping all my children in the shower...soap opera.

Your momma should have choked poppa with a lifestyle rubber for faking real porn. That night, you should have never moved down your daddy's pipe, or at birth you should have died as a baby...still born.

We can do this like gangsters and thugs and pull off the gloves because I'm not your friend, your partner, your pal, your homey, your crony or your cuz. Truthfully, you gets no love. I'm not your fam, or your brother from another mother, and honestly, I'd poison my veins and slit my own wrists if I ever found out we were the same blood.

I'm an addictive drug like Freddy Krueger taking sleeping pills...and for a hot second I been killing the scene like a cameo. I'm hotter than a humpback beast in the summer and you just a pussy in tight jeans...camel toe. Working it out, exercising these demons with lyrical schemes to have no love handles, hoe. I'm strickly Ol' Skool like vice grips on TVs, you have to turn three clicks just to play this game and see me...or channel four.

I used to run laps around beaches like you in the sand until my sandals broke and would still pull your girl, in a smart car looking like Ashy Anne. I'll make her a genius on this penis, knowledgeable, giving good brain so I can call her the smart Kardashian.

Lyrical Punishment

Somebody better go call the law cause I'm about to punish this man. Three minutes to drop more lyrical bombs than father and son George Bush, Bin Laden and the Taliban.

I spit more fire than a two-headed dragon with hair like Medusa with a cold to heat, burn and beat ya. I'm that lyrical beast, or like the Loch ness monster, I'm not just a youngster or your average Sea Serpent creature.

Putting poets to death like the grim reaper, I bang on my chest like King Kong with a Big Foot, with that gold missing link on my chain for a charm, so don't you ever step to me son. I'm the boogieman of poetry; I stroll through Jurassic Park like the Ape man on a unicorn on a full moon and scare the shit out of werewolves, vampires and leprechauns.

Using my giant Cyclops to molest the minds of the mermaids in the ponds while I search for Godzilla with no help from my poetic friends. Then, take off my shirt in the winter with a snow cone and microphone in hand and show you who the real Abdominal Snowman is.

Taking on the swamp monster, Sasquach, and two midget twins. Shit, I wouldn't even give a damn if you tagged team with Harry and the Hendersons.

Me habla en Espaniol et Je parle Francais, nigga I'll battle you in two other different languages. Cause my flow is out of this world, I spit a piece and translated it myself, then wrecked E.T., Alf and two different aliens.

Making waves way in the Caribbean cause anything below the best clashes with my old school swagger and demeanor. I once sat with Shakespeare puffing on the magic dragon and told him to make Beowulf a little meaner.

I'm colder than a frozen freezer; so you can see smoke when I speak and blow and when I spit my saliva turns into icicles. Using the power of my tongue to bully you and take a bite of the booty of your sour pickle.

And you probably wouldn't do nothing but giggle, but on the inside, you bitch, moan and complain. Even if I were the all great and powerful Oz I'd just consume your thoughts like the blob, would never grant you a damn brain.

Cause I see ya the type of lame ass that needs help on the shit you spit so you get with other poets and try to collaborate. Nigga, I do my shit the way I like my drinks with no sweet juice, like a real player just straight not gay.

Seducing all women with seductive verses and foreplay to make the area between their legs moisten and cream. Turning nightmares about Freddy Krueger into wet dreams and celibate virgins practicing abstinence into nymphomaniacs that rape sex fiends.

Making me the next man mean enough to just steal the air from your lips with my words as they rip while you gasp for your last breath. Then, check you into the coroner's office just so your autopsy can prove that an overload of riddle and rhyme caused a brain tumor which was the main cause of death.

So with about one minute left, I'm going to dig your grave and put nails in the casket. Matter of fact, I'm going to throw the mic in there with you with a few verses that are drastic, cause you can have it.

I play devil's advocate when I make my quill bleed ink then hold it still after scratching verses on the fabric of my paper. Making my number two pencil jealous because suspenseful words were pressed up and permanently left on the paper with that quill, leaving scars on it for later.

I ain't never been a hater so when I'm finished you can take my pencil home so you can use it as a magic utensil to write something fast and suspenseful just so you'll feel a little better. Better yet I take that back. I wouldn't care if you were a lost poodle standing alone in a blizzard thunderstorm with no master or a sweater.

I'm not Rhianna, bitch and not your friend so I'mma finish this cause I wouldn't dare let you stand under my umbrella. I'd ride by the curb and splash you with a few more watery sarcastic words written together with my finger out the window hollering I'm sorry I had to do this, so have a nice day but fuck you young feller.

Male Bash

I can't believe you got the nerve to try to male bash. You roachin' and penny pinchin' hoe. You wearing your friends' clothes and out there trying to sell ass.

You ain't worth a brown blade of stale grass that I step out the car to piss and throw up on when I leave the club at night. Worrying why you can't find a decent man. That's because all you want is a thug in your life.

Wondering why nobody will love you right. Telling your girls all you attract is dogs, and you keep getting your feelings involved, and these niggas ain't shit. Look in the mirror. You're the one club hopping and pussy popping showing your ass looking like New York trash, so maybe you need to just stop being a bitch.

I can see you just another gold digger trick trying to get treats with some more bullshit get rich quick schemes. Talking about, "Girl once I whip this good pussy on him, he's going to buy me everything that blings."

You get what you deserve, so don't even worry about what justice is. A man is only what you make him out to be and you're only what you show him you are so why fake like it ain't is what it is.

It's said that when it rains it pours and when it pours it floods. But when a poor man reigns and eyes flood with pain, you still have no shame to kick him down in the mud.

And you want to get the point understood that you're an independent woman. Down talking other women saying these hoes ain't shit, but bitch you just need to stop fronting.

Stop asking and wanting everybody else to help you and take care of your problems. Stop whining, get your shit together, your own car, own house, pay your own bills or just show some initiative and will, and a man might help you solve 'em.

Stupid is a choice, so you just so happen to choose to be stupid. It's your choice to be foolish and deal with these ruthless ass men that don't do shit but plant a seed inside your two lips or give you a huge dick to use as a toothpick, so stop bitching and trying to find a reason to cuss out cupid.

You knew this shit was going happen when you met him. He used you, fucked you, abused you, then left you, and you let him.

Baby, you're supposed to be the master of your own fate and the captain of your soul. But instead you let the actions of one man dictate your actions toward another, so any other man is left out in the cold.

Saying this bold ass shit, like all men ain't no good. Bitch, I work, I cook, I clean spilled milk off the floor with a 700 plus credit score out of the hood, got my own shit, eat a barrel of pussy like a pack of pink starburst, with a big black dick, and I look and fuck good.

So let's just get this shit understood cause I know I'm not the last of a dying breed. All the niggas I fuck with take care of their kids, handle they business and still don't mind helping a woman in need.

Not just another woman on her knees but a woman that has some ambition and wants something out of life. Maybe, if you change your bitching ass attitude, you might find a decent man that'll treat you right.

Someone that doesn't mind buying you nice things out of the goodness of his heart. But if that's your hidden agenda, I hope you get fucked and cussed out from the start.

I hope he marches all over your feelings with shitty steel-toed boots. Maybe, then you'd get the picture to stop trying to play men with ulterior motives to get their loot.

And I know the dark truth hurts, so I don't mind telling you a lil bit more. Stop being the bitch a nigga fuck with when his bitch ain't fucking with him like a lil' hoe because just because you fuck and suck a man dick don't mean he has to pay the buck or try to even the score.

You, of all people, should know you can't turn a hoe into a housewife. That ain't nothing but another statistic and a lost life.

Man, that cost might cost a man too much in his life he can deal with. And I don't know any man that will ever settle with a real bitch.

So get this, if you have to be a bitch or a hoe, it's better to have a man call you one because you did none of the shit asked. You don't even deserve the audacity to get mad, because after you've done everything he asked, he's going to still going to call you a hoe or a bitch after he got that ass.

You have to stop giving yourself up to someone if you don't even know who you are. If you applied your common sense to your everyday living, not anything in this life could ever stop you from going far.

I think a dog doesn't become a real man 'til he loses a good woman. And a good woman doesn't become a real bitch 'til she's been with a dog. So if you treat him right from the start, you'd be treated right from his heart and your problems might be dissolved.

And since you got the federal government involved, apparently you may not be as good a parent because they saw twenty percent to fit and be sufficient to aid in the support for a child. But it's not to pay for flat ironed synthetic multi-weave wet and wavy Yaky #9 hairstyles and Chinese nail files. It's meant to be compiled with your twenty percent, so deal with it, lose that stank attitude and stop being so hostile.

But I know you're probably going to be out here trying to stay awhile and file child support on another brother, putting price tags on men as long as the sale lasts. So, my advice for you is to keep your opinions to yourself the next time you ever try to waste your stale breath to male bash.

Yes I think you deserve to die and I hope you burn in hell tonight. This is Ol' Skool, now imagine that she is white.

Ol Skool

Damn near everywhere I go people wonder about my Ol Skool name and where I get this cool ass swagger I always seem to maintain. Shit, I usually jus tell them I grew up around old crack heads, ex-tricks, and convicts in the projects, but tonight I'm going to show you the roots of my ol skool name.

I'm ol skool like we ain't got no more milk so we goin to mix this cereal and water. And back in the gap when you had a fight, yo mamma said 'if you don't win Imma whoop yo ass' so it made you fight a little harder.

And if I did lose, or for any other reason, I got my ass beat in syllables while she held me by one hand and ran around in the grass. I'm ol skool like "don't let them streetlights catch ya" or "go cut me a switch cause Imma bout to beat yo nappy headed black ass."

I'm ol skool like afros and picks with the fists, or cornrows and high-top fades. Shit, I'm ol skool like activator and jerry curls in that plastic bag, or cutting the foot out of momma's stockings for a stocking cap and putting it on your head at night to take care of the finger waves.

I'm ol skool like peanut butter and syrup sandwiches, or using an iron and brown paper bag to make a fast grill cheese. Shit, I'm ol skool like putting today's outfit between the mattresses to get that razor sharp crease that morning before hitting the streets.

Ol skool like 227, Sanford and Son, Good Times, Different Strokes, and Amen giving out the good news. I'm black like Sicily Tyson and Harry Bellefonte, or even Sydney Portier or Billy Dee Williams in Lady Sings the Blues.

I'm ol skool like the females always wanting that light skinned or mixed nigga with the baby hairs that be thinking he too damn pretty. Or overweight females saying they ain't fat they just big boned, or lying they ass off saying they got good hair talking about "Bitch I got Indian in the family."

Knowing damn well that ain't nothing but an Ultra perm. I'm talking about that book of food stamps we used to get or in school using that meal ticket and everybody was scared to fight that nigga everybody thought was fruity. Shit, I'm ol skool like buying a pickle and putting a peppermint in it or asking somebody else for a bite of the booty.

Ol skool like Daisy Dukes and Coochie Cutters, or Dookie braids, Pin Curl pony tails and Swoops. I'm ol skool like babies in diapers outside with no shoes or calling three feet when you're shooting hoops.

Ol skool like hoola-hooping around the neck then big momma always coming outside holding her overcoat closed with one finger and her wig cocked to the side tripping. I used to have a mountain bike back tire, Shwinn frame, Redline front tire with bull brakes pumping my nigga on the Huffy handle bars. I'm v like nigga riggin'.

Ol skool like that little TV that sat on top of the big TV and you had to use grip pliers just to turn it. I'm ghetto black like shooting dice in the alley, wall ball, double dutch and slap boxing while the grown folks played spades and we sneaked off to play hide-n-go get it.

Ol skool like cross colors and fat laced Pumas with that fresh step cut into that box fade and the three parts on the side and all the hoes was jockin'. Shit, I'm ol skool like running around at two in the morning from door to door and we all called it nigga knocking'.

Ol skool like smothered pork chops, rice and gravy, collard greens, yams, catfish, and Creole gumbo. I'm ghetto like red kool-aid or when it got too hot in the summer we used to sing aaahh into the fan in the window.

I'm talking about MD 20/20, Red Bull, White Lightning, Sisco, Thunderbird and Night Train living up the life. I'm ol skool like putting your chin to the bottom of a cool cup to turn it over and suck the juice out right.

And even if it fell to the ground it was God kiss it, devil miss it, or God made dirt and dirt don't hurt and wiping it off on your clothes. I'm ol skool The Wiz, The Last Dragon, Colors and Penitentiary 1, 2 ,and 3 where Two Sweet took on all the prison foes.

I'm talking about going five on the weed with four niggas sipping' on a forty posted up on the corner with no shame. I'm ol skool like watching Donnie Simpson and Video Soul or Don Cornelius and Soul Train.

Or making fun of that wino singing in the rain or ranking on each other saying, "You ain't got a pot to piss in or a window to throw it out." I'm ol skool football in the street before school and having grass stain cause we called it sideline pop.

And when a dope ride rode by on some fresh rims we all yelled bingo. I'm ol skool like will you go with me? Circle yes, maybe, or no.

On the Rag

This is my monthly cycle. Every 28 days, with wings, I always give my pen a pad when my pencil's on the rag and starting its menstrual just so I can absorb the ink that bleeds from my writing utensil because it's known to make a female suspenseful and drawers get so wet. That was the first panty liner. Kotex.

But, at the end, there's no period near this mental pause. Just a continual discharge of rhythm and rhyme that intoxicates lots of dates like Moet. Don't believe me? Just watch your clock. Rolex.

I write the internal pain that drains your particular way of living with a smile. Meaning my calligraphy cramps your style or like a tramp in the wild in heat, lusting for mo' sex, I'm working it out with strength to make the blood rush. Bowflex.

And I keep tampons for the hopeless hating damp ones that are spotted throughout this cycle of menstruation that silently leak out and protest. I don't need the light or the mic. Like a stampede of bulls, my words are heard and my voice is bright enough to project. I'm backed up by a long list of writers that love to manipulate words and inspire others. Poets.

Something serious. When I'm on my period, I get delirious with the rigorousness like retards with down syndrome driving below speed limits in a show vet, taking their time to bump and grind. Slow sex.

There's no stopping this menstrual flow. With blood on these sheets, there's no love in the streets and nothing can shield you from the massacre and mayhem or keep you out of harm's way. Protect.

I spit venom to demons and convert mental slaves to free men in ways that would make you think I had hands of healing that were held by angels. So blessed.

Power Of My Words

Some motherfucker once told me that the strength of my words was not powerful. And that my thought process behind the shit I spit may even seem doubtful. So I tell you what, after I read this I'mma tattoo this piece to the shaft of my penis just to be thoughtful so you can believe this and I hope its unlawful when I unzip these thoughts on my head you can open wide and get a whole mouthful.

Man like vaporizing a bull with a small marble I can paralyze your mind in time with a simple parable then lay your thoughts out on a stretcher and then stabilize you with that same variable. Put you in a daze with a crippled phrase and then hypnotize you into thinking you got it made as a black slave in a Mississippi Cotton Bowl parade.

More quicker than bullets and tumors, the shit I spit can hit quicker than bad rumors that beat you home. And can even measure up to the strength in big momma's voice when she says, "Boy, if you don't get yo' ass off that damn phone."

And I know you've heard the phrase "stick and stones may break my bones, but words will never hurt me." That's some bullshit because sticks and stones are temporary wounds but the force of my verbs can punish and bruise your soul and hurt internally for eternity.

Powerful like that referee that throws in the towel and says stop the fight. And maybe as mighty as a simple 'I love you' or the magic in God's words when shattered the dark and said 'let there be light.'

I can cause fright in even the bravest of men like that werewolf that terrorized the streets of Paris and strolled through the alleys of London even with that scary, mad song sung. Damn that, my words have more vigor to cause more heartbreak or more fear like that broken Magnum condom.

Like Magic Don Juan I can commit grand theft thought so I have the ability to steal your mind. And believe my word is bond when I deepen my voice I have the ability to send chills up a woman's spine.

Cause even with a high and cloudy mind I can converse lyrical verses of seduction to your intellectual and through the cloudiness let my words disperse and just rain out. Giving me the power to make love to a female's mind right before I bend her over and fuck her brains out.

Fabricating her body to moisten and weaken as she sits there and listens. My words are mighty like the words in St. Paul's letters that he wrote that became the New Testament while he was in prison.

You see, even when she was missing the potency my words became my mother's main remedy and ointment that kept her sane while she was in jail. And if any one of you motherfuckers piss me off, I can verbally attack and assault you to leave more bumps, lumps and bruises than the balled up pages thrown against the wall from an angry blind man's book of Braille.

You can even hear me if I didn't scream or yell and you were deaf because my voice carries volumes. Even if you were a baby screaming, the frequencies of my whispers would be the magic force that shut you the fuck up and calm you.

Warming you in the coldest of weather, my words consist of letters that are treasured from a first love. My words are powerful enough to end the killing war of the worlds between the crips and bloods.

I have the endowment to make a man think and know he can, even when he thought he couldn't. The things I say can stop a child back in the day who said anything about your momma avoid that ass whooping.

And having even the sad laughing and hooting, cause the way I manipulate and play with words makes them calm and relaxed. I can give a headache to Excederin and knock the shit out of Ex-lax.

Fuck that, I put fear in a gorilla and can make him bow down and twitch. I can make you more worried than when you got into trouble and you had to take that long walk when your mother told you "Boy, get your ass up and go and cut me a switch."

More robust than her saying I'm doing this because I love you. More sarcastic than her lying ass renigging and saying this is going to hurt me more than it hurts you.

Do you remember when some words when you said them made you feel cool? I thought I pulled the dope game and had the dope moves when I used funky fresh and fly after watching the newest episode of the Fresh Prince of Bel-aire when I was in school.

I must have been a fool to think that shit. But, my words have no limits because they can be worse and more cold-blooded than the neighborhood snitch. Fuck that, they're fiercer than that rage felt as a child when someone called your momma a bitch.

Even like the Willie Lynch letter, I can control slaves' minds and keep order by turning them against themselves without even using whips. With my power of persuasion, I can tell a female what to say if she ever wants to get licked and have her man's tongue turn as hard as woodpecker lips.

So just remember, as a poet, I am very sensitive about the shit I spit. My words can even be more powerful and demanding than the amazing sensations of a woman's clit.

Even if you put a censorship over the words from my lips like on a TV clip, you can still understand the shit I spit when you see my scattered finger whip through the air and my jaws clench and twitch before my lips grip and say (fuck you bitch). And I'm through with this shit.

Reason To Hate Me

  Bitch, you're so fucking far beneath me your absolute motherfucking best is filthy rags. Your tongue stank so much from mumbling shit to yourself under your breath from your ass it's probably potent enough to make a starving maggot and Billy goat gag.

  Nigga, I'm a trash shit talker, ass night stalker by nature. This is the type of shit I excel very well in. When I'm up here, it's only the light, me and the mic so you and any other hating mother fucker ain't nothing but another hoe ass ad lib.

  I spit more wisdom than a half-drunken old wise man tongue-tied even with that wisdom tooth gone. The shit you saying is like a puppy chewing shoes slobbering just young getting your drool on like a motherfucking toothless newborn.

  Nigga, they call me Ol' Skool but this a new poem giving you access to my life so how in the fuck are you going to criticize me and the shit I spit about whether drunk or not when I bless this stage. I unleash words and concepts from a vocabulary that's caged up in a rage and I am never afraid to release and tame them when I put pen to page.

  I don't just write poetry, bitch, I'm a fucking poet. Anybody can write punch lines with similes and metaphors that that rhyme, but I can make the microphone cry, moist, laugh and curse or go sweat from heated seductive lyrical verses from a sex piece to make a female so wet.

  And you know it. So go get your thesauruses and dictionary when I decide to verbalize and spit flowing molten lava from this dry volcanic ash boiling inside my mind. I chew up devastation, digest the truth, belch reality, fart pride, and can still find time to shit out lies like a snitching convicted felon on deferred judification after coughing up the street code, telling and turning states' evidence on nine capital crimes.

  Making my soul cry and at the same time making you an indentured servant of mine that sweats jealousy and bleeds envy under the blistering heat of words that's ripped and torn from pages of my rhyme book. I'll give you a reason to hate me like the way women hate a crooked dick that's hooked and won't stay up then do it again like déjà vu so if you missed me the first time you'd be shook and have a good clue to steal a second look.

  Just to have your sorry ass face hook, drop, drag and hang low as sagging tiddies or flies in shit house buckets. Bitch, you could never do what I do. My words carry life like a stretcher and I bet you I can do a different piece a week and shove 'em out for years and would never give a good got damn motherfucker whether you hate it or love it.

So fuck it, because you don't even know the process behind this shit I spit when I decide to get up to rip this bitch. And any poet can vouch for this shit. Create a new concept. Find a twist. Take a few notes. Make time for days to write and rewrite the shit. And even more days to re-write and recite the shit. Use a little more time to re-write for the right delivery to spit. Then get here early enough with a forty-five minute drive to put my motherfucking name on the list. All for your ignorant ass to criticize this shit.

Bitch, please. I don't give a good fuck how it makes you feel, just so you know. If my dick was my name it stays in your mouth and I hope you swallow the words from my brain till you gag and choke.

Cause this shit wasn't wrote for applause, praise, props or popularity. I do this shit to get my motherfucking points across and to free myself to give my mind some got damn clarity.

I take the fear in me, love, hate, sorrows, dreams, ambition and escape to a world where I ball and suppress them up in the pits of my stomach with all of my might. Pressure busts a pipe so I let them explode through the ink and let the words ignite, disperse and freely scatter. Shit, I'm stripping myself of my own got damn powers on this night just by addressing you and this motherfucking matter.

I'd rather just spit these hollow point lyrical bullets into my own hands than to waste the gunpowder embedded in my lungs just to shoot you. I ought to just grab you by your throat and pull you to the shells and make your mind the target to poke, shove and just mash 'em through you.

Nigga, I will do you in and rule you if you ever got something to say about me or some shit I speak about that will piss me off so remember you can never make me or break me. I'm fueled by your energy and could care less about another motherfucking enemy so I'm giving you a better reason to hate me.

So do what you do and let it be done when you do it, you sorry ass bitch. I said that. Meant that. And the motherfucking me fight go with that shit. Now say something or do something about the shit I spit so your face can get broken. Or just shut your motherfucking mouth next time you hear grown folks talking, you young dumb punk, because your boy Ol' Skool has just spoken.

Heathenism

On to the next heathen…bona-fied nympho-maniacle sex demon…Ol' Skool's a certified diabolical vet scheming to chronicle women's deep chest breathing while sleeping and dilute every moist molecule from wet dreaming with phenomenal sweat leaking from every follicle that's peeking through the flesh to make it sensual, yet ironical, just seeping through the pores while on all fours to make it the best probable season for sexual healing.

A known night stalker and shit talker in any establishment with an everlasting twitch…and filthy mouth with a mustache of lint screaming blasphemous that you can have this shit, giving my last two cents to pass as rent which is probably the cash you spent without me even asking it.

So I just need you to bypass the French and bask in it as I poison and contaminate your cerebral with galactic spit because I'm known to do more than enough to too much with a pen and pad. And if this is a sin, I'm glad I can't be touched, I just grin when mad…and wouldn't give a good fuck if you luck up to win or sad.

The words from above my chin are bad, but I maintain a cool temperament with more than enough evidence of it. My mind's depth and common sense is ten percent of infinite with definite instruments to disturb any turbulence. So, when pissed off, I murder this or squirt the piss at any worthless shit and I make sure the words exist to hurt or diss.

I can be the purest kiss that turns you on at night. I am the great risk that most are willing to take when most things aren't going right.

I am nothing and everything. The hope…the great what IF. The dead man's body as the spirit uplifts.
I am a chip off the old block, better known with a chip on my shoulder. The first breeze felt when the weather gets colder.

A subliminal message on a poster for imposters to conceive. A note between a note that you would never believe. Close calls I don't have them. But I will call your bluff. It appears to me anyone will always be too little, not enough.

My tough path is made of quick sand, so you're bound to sink deep. My smile and eyes only hide my most powerful weapon which lies behind my teeth. With that being said, I sit calmly at my throne.

A heathen…with heathenistic characteristics…a PHD in Heathenology…living in a state of heathenism deep within the system.

Born and bred this way, caged enraged in a prism for no sensible reason…a sex tool for sex fiends with wet dreams, sexing extreme with me in their next scheme for the best cream for teasing and pleasing.

A master of the arts of sensual seduction, mental corruption, and parental discussions rated-X about butt naked sex. I am Ol' Skool. A damn fool. Yet so cool that most women get wet and drool then take bets over what I might say next when I began to rule.

Trifling Hoes

This is for them trifling ass hoes. For them penny pinching and roachin don't want to do the right thing ass hoes.

Can't see the lightning from the flash in your eyes. Want to talk bout me and shit but in the club with your friend's outfit pretending it's yours in disguise.

Telling lies just fronting. I'm getting mine and got mine and you want to be my gal so why you bumping.

I know your kind. Go out just on ladies' night broke dressed for the bed posted up by the bar in hopes of a nigga buying that fine wine.

Thinking you 'bout to get mine. Bitch, you must be tripping. I'm talking about the type of hoe that's in the club wearing a g-string on her period.

Damn near dripping portraying a clash of flash like she got cash and class with much pazass. You ain't really nothing but some other nigga's future baby mother trying to trap him with child support in the club showing her ass.

Trying to get mad at me with a shitty attitude. Wanting niggas to sleep with you on your period. Oh, yeah I can tell by your mood.

Bitch, I got a habit for being rude to hoes that think they're too much. You the type that will open a box of Tampax in the store and use it, even if it costs one buck.

Just fucking nasty. Thinking you just the finest thing on the block. In public looking so trashy with stretch marks on your belly looking like abstract art.

Don't nobody want to see that shit. You'se a three-time knock up getting child support trying to fuck for the rent.

House probably just as filthy as you look. Clothes scattered everywhere when company comes over talking about 'excuse the mess' with dirty ass dishes telling me it's been a while since anybody cooked.

You ain't nothing but a part time crook about to run smooth out of luck. I'm talking a trifling ass hoe that will put her own child out just to get a quick fuck.

Just stuck on stupid. You'd probably go on fucking niggas knowing that you had a disease whether they can or can not cure it.

Gold digging just looking at how much money you can get out of a man. Doing anything you can to try and trap that man to get some child support from that man.

One of the best lying and trifling actors. Pussy so funky and nasty they wouldn't allow that shit on Fear Factor.

You the type that will start a new chapter that would poke a hole in a rubber. Or pick a used one out the gutter and get caught and still try to lie with a straight face and no stutter plotting on that brother.

There ain't any other nigga I know that will put up with some bullshit like that on any day in the week. I shouldn't have to go in your bathroom and smell the sex on a towel left on the damn sink.

Or see pubic hair abandoned under the toilet seat when I raise it to urinate. Why in the hell would you leave a piss stain on it knowing someone might notice the display?

Do you have no shame? When you turn on the lights in your house roaches shouldn't scatter like droplets of rain.

It pains me to just say I know who you are and there are many like you. This is dedicated to them trifling ass hoes and if you fit the description this is probably you.

Truth and Bullshit

A long time ago I discovered that the truth could bleed through the ink from my pen to pad to page from cover to cover of any book and rage like no other. And like a blind man's finger print, no one has my kind of sense, and I was always trying to be different from the next brother.

From diapers to depends, my mother or even folks that are not my friends could tell you that I'm destined for total greatness. I spit truth, no in-betweens and no bullshit as if I was allergic to lies, so if you hate this, tell me the truth because I'm abstaining and celibate from fakeness.

So all I ask is that you take this piece of mind and run with it till the end of time as I shatter the glass on any haters. I am the great debater, so you want to get at me later, I'll be glad to be your waiter and serve you up some bullshit to poison your mind like a high treason traitor.

Truth is, like a starving gator, I chew up bullshit and spit it back to the creator in riddle and rhyme in ways to paralyze the mind. I can even stabilize a politician's true lies in ways that the bullshit is lost in a wrinkle in time.

So with that same state of mind, I'm going to tell you the truth; yes, most men do cheat and lie. Some lie so much their truth is bullshit and the excuses they give when they use it are also camouflaged with pride in disguise.

But the bullshit part about it is that women tend to forget the fact that they lie and cheat to. Truth is, most just never get caught. And most men are so naive into a bullshit state of mind so they tend to think that they lay so much good dick their woman would never deceive them.

Like I told you, I'm here to speak the truth. Because I know for a fact that a man and a woman can truly love each other with all their heart. Bullshit part about it is the fact that they can also fuck another with no heart and keep their feelings apart while still loving each other as they did from the start.

My main mission is to struggle and dig through the bullshit to find the truth. So here's some more true shit. I got a partner that wasn't even slow or stupid, but was put into a special education class when he was a kid. Bullshit part about it was the fact that his grandmother was just trying to get a free check, so that was the main reason she did the bullshit she did.

Most things that are true are always surrounded by lies and bullshit. Maybe bullshit is the antidote for truth if no one wants to take the time to acknowledge it.

I mean, we know the true fact that Michael Vick was charged and sentenced for dog fights. Bullshit part about that is a white woman received less time than him after shooting her husband in cold blood who was a preacher. She just got 210 days for taking his raw life.

It seems that we deal and tend to accept more bullshit than truths everyday. Truth is, most if not all of these sorry ass niggas deserve to have child support put on their ass. Bullshit part about it is that most women put it on them, not because he's not a father to his child, but because of the true fact that he got away from her bullshit and left her sorry ass.

Because the truth is, I don't know too many men that will not take care and responsibility for their child. It's just that most have to go through so much bullshit to see their child that it's hard for a nigga to try to stay for awhile.

Most of the time, the absolute truth is bullshit. Yet, it is always neglected. Truth is condoms are needed; but the bullshit part about it is the fact that most relationships don't use them and they are mostly getting tested and results come up infected.

And you can reject it, all the bull shit if you want, but the truth is what I'm after. And I will tell the truth; yes, most men do just want to fuck. Bullshit part about that is the fact that most women don't tell the truth because they just want to fuck too.

They run around talking about size doesn't matter when the truth is that it does. Bullshit part about it is the fact that most can't handle a big piece of meat anyway when push comes to shove.

Truth is most are more worried about what they look like and their weight. When the bullshit part about it, is the fact that there is always someone around that will fuck on any day.

There are approximately 127 million adults in the US that are overweight and 60 million are obese. Bullshit part about that is the fact the there are only slim people working out in the gyms living at peace.

And before I release myself from the thought process, I want to leave you with this last piece of mind. Truth is that there are a lot of drunk drivers in the world. Bullshit part about that is the fact that they are not the ones dying. Instead it's the other car's fathers, mothers, sons, and little girls.

Won't Be Defeated

This is my refusal. Even though I feel watched and cheated, I will not be defeated. And though I get a little hot and heated, been blocked and mistreated, I won't stop and believe it, that I'm like a lot that don't need it. I see clear in HD, so picture it, crop and perceive it; I will drop to my knees if I got to achieve it because I am destined for God's greatness.

And at all odds I take this with open hands, even though sometimes it doesn't make sense like hoping plans to drown between two different wavelengths is better than being body-slammed on two different pavements. To me it's the same, at least you live to face it.

So take this, I don't waste cents. For breakfast, I eat patience because I hate grits and fake shit that's time consuming and the show gets so hopeless. I was breaking myself down trying to fix other people's broke shit, but I gained more strength and knowledge from fuck-ups so I didn't turn into one that's so roguish and slowish that drowns in his own cold piss.

So focus, even if you are hoe-ish, I really just want to make sure you know this. Sometime you have to play dumb when folks play stupid, just to see how much of a useless fool they take you for. People won't see your strengths because it's blocked behind their insecurities and their weaknesses and that's probably the reason they hate you more.

I don't care what you rate the score. I require less than I desire, gain less than I expect, and give all that I have, but am still required and expected to smile laugh as I give more. I've been rejected by those I love and loved by those I barely even know as if I was some promiscuous prostitute at a free show or a real whore that's still poor. But I don't complain; it's life.

And I feel more like in a time of universal deceit, telling the truth becomes a revolutionary act. And it's so hard for you to grasp and accept that concept of the truth and fact when the lies were exactly what you wanted to hear, even when behind your back.

Men need to stop thinking every woman is a good digger because she likes the finer things in life and stop just assuming she's spoiled. And women need to stop looking for a knight in shining armor because it's probably just some fool claiming to be doing it all wrapped in aluminum foil.

And instead of choosing to boil, maybe I should be as cold as ice and give you a dose of life as a poltergeist that composed a plight of the coldest heist that chose to bite at an open mic. A nigga couldn't see me at a closer sight if I rode a bike to a show tonight. I'd just approach him right to hold him tight and choke his life with my chosen type of scrotum vice or hold a knife and poke him twice when we were supposed to fight.

But instead of going on that hopeless flight, I'm as bold as Christ, keeping it slow and nice below the nights as I control the price to be paid and mice to be sprayed in my life that I've paved at my own discretion.

I've made it my own lesson and I refuse to be defeated. I'd rather lose and be beaten, then used and eaten than choose to be deleted from a bruise that I needed to leave me confused and retreated.

I mean, being abused and mistreated *is* what keeps me razor sharp like a hick blade at a trailer park. And though it may be dark in this world of sin, I still grin like a killer whale or shark on a sailor's heart when the flavor's tart and the wave's apart.

I know my days are short in a room of fuses, but, at will, I still ignite and convey the spark so I can cause that boom of contusions.

A Long Walk

She said she wanted to take a long walk with me…to talk with me. I just guessed she wanted to see what instinctive predatory moves I would use to stalk and hover above her thoughts, so she could see the starving hawk in me.

Truly, I just had this perverse fascination with her inner workings. To bring a sort of serenity and calm to whatever was hurting. You see, it is what it is at the time that it was, so now that it ain't, I had to stop her from trying to go back to what it never would be. I wanted to show her what it should be.

What it could be if we were to just let go of all inhibition while we're in this position to do so. As a man, it's never been a part of the plan to cruise slow, but instead, move low and take this long walk down lover's lane.

And I could see it running through her brain, I kind of figured that she knew my background wasn't squeaky clean; that I had a reputation for sexual persuasion and seducing women into giving up that leaky thing.

But that really wasn't my objective with this lady. On this walk, while the sky was still dark and hazy, my main mission and disposition was relaxation and mental stimulation. I really just wanted us to discuss this situation.

And as love was racing to one destination, it was mind bending, crime ending, our hearts became a window for our soul's indo. It was music that trembled. Our feet were the tempo, kicking like Kenpo, no info was sinful, but each verse was a pen stroke that was like a simple demo to win more dimples that stretched from temple to temple across her face. We were elevated at this dark place lit up by each other's smile. I could tell she wanted me to stay for a while. I turn to play and say I couldn't stay but she just said come on, come.

Dominance

All of a sudden, and with no hesitation, my hands are racing to chase in between the space to reach that patch of flesh of your neck. Tonight, I *am* taking your sex, and I can now feel your pounding pulse as I pull you nearer than close, like shadows in mid-pirouettes in the mirror, exposed, engaging in a slow dance with tempting silhouettes.

But, unlike second-hand smoking from loose cigarettes, I'm not choking you. Just holding you as I kiss you so passionately, so deeply, provoking you to forget whose air you've been actually breathing and stealing like a thief in the late night. So I sink my teeth in, with a great bite, forcing blurred and hazy sights and that pulsating muscle to contract and get wetter and moist than a brand-new flooded bucket of baby wipes.

And, I can feel that lower lady bite, looking like a swollen bicep from angry fights between your hips and thighs. I love the way it grips when wide. Like sex weed, I prefer to smoke on my knees so I can tongue kiss it high and taste your fountain of praise that I worship like a graced gift from gods.

You see, when you speak, you only repeat what you already know, but when you listen, you may hear something you may have been missing from the show and learn something new. So, shut the hell up, and let me do what I do. The beast comes out when least expected, so when it does come out, don't blame the beast that's been selected, put blame on the hunted because it's no longer an endangered species to be protected.

The Lion King is in the room for good and I will strategically impale you with this polished wood and devour you like a fat rat. Master Splinter. I'm a pit bull trying to get full, and you are what I want to have for dinner. And, after it's tender, I'm tasting all your sex parts till my tongue stiffens or gets stretch marks, whether it's bald, trimmed or even if the grass is thicker.

Forget the sex tonight, this malnourished, dehydrated more than average nigga is in that hot and humid sauna between your legs draining you out your electrolytes, sipping on that sweet juice from within you, and if I have to, I'll even chase it with a Patron shot and a glass of liquor as if it's squirting succulent wine from a classic vineyard.

Gripping your lavish figure in a way to make that ass surrender just like the last contender, and I won't even stop if my tonsils cramp out or my jaw hurts. Munching on that cookie like the last perfect packaged pack of pink Starburst. If illegal, I'd break the law first or just flat out pay for it…cash dispenser. Clitoris flipping and tongue dipping, mad and quicker, like the legs from the adrenaline rush of Usain Bolt, the fastest sprinter.

But, first allow this nice dude to make you gasp and shiver as I take an ice cube clenched between my teeth to crash it in between the lips to your inner core's heat to simulate Jurassic winter. And, even though it's already a little colder than the past December, I'll go on ahead and plant my feet with a slow dip in my hip to go knee deep in your sizzling swamps, so it feels like my calf was in ya. Slipping nothing but head and neck past the center of the lotus leaves to your sacred tree so my hot and primitive, chocolate giraffe can enter. Forcing the short breaths of air of every moan you bear to sound exactly like when inhaled from laughing inward.

Now, do what I told you to do and bend over the armrest of your own sofa so I get all the luck I can get out of that two-leaf clover. This is the battle of Saratoga, and I want to see if all that yoga you've been doing and kegalistic-constricting of that boa can tame this cobra. It's as wet as the sweat on an ice cold can of Coca Cola on a park bench in Arizona. While you're pushing and gripping clothes, I got you on your tippy toes as my throbbing head has its one eye swinging hard and lower to that swollen, juicy fist like when Harpo hit Oprah.

Lifting, touching, and gripping you in places you forgot even existed, I need to fulfill my quota of forcing the supernova of your chocolate mocha biscuit in that heated space to fizz, quick like when you mix vinegar and baking soda, and I plan to do just what I said. I flip you over, gradually resting your calf muscles on upon my shoulder while my tongue cruises over the epidermis of your legs, but I stop to lick and suck on your toes, instead.

To be continued…

Got That Wood

Now, how much wood would a woodchuck fuck, if a woodchuck would suck wood? Every time you see me, you can go ahead and stand beneath me, so I can call you Miss Understood.

Don't worry. It's juicy and thickened like a baby's leg and polished like it's been sprayed with Pledge. I swing a thunder axe like a lumberjack and you can believe it's a fact when I say that I'm coming back with the Razor's Edge.

I pack that high quality wood. I'm talking about that top notch pine. That four-by-nine is sublime and my timber is hot like a cinderblock and when I chop, I'm known to just splint the spot.

I'll have you riding the pine like a third-string player, screaming 'it's going down' like a tree in Himalaya. And I'll yell, 'Tiiiiiimmmmmbbbeerrr' when I'm within her, every time I get you in my lair.

Smoother than Nair, baby, it is smoke tan and way better than a coke can. I can be your wood-ologist spokesman. Not even Smokey the Bear can put out your forest fire, but I guarantee this wet oak can.

So, go ahead and get in the car before you start dripping rain. We can go as far as you can, just start gripping grain. I'll nail this wood up in your neighborhood just like iron in the tracks of a freight train.

It's a heavy weight 'thang'. Big lumber packing, just like Jim Dugan. If I stepped up to bat I'd be Louisville sluggin'.

And all our raw lust would be the saw dust. I wouldn't give a damn whoever saw us.

I lay good wood like a carpenter. African Hardwood, nothing is harder, girl. Even a pipe laying plumber would be left in a slumber and wouldn't ever want to go to war with us.

Keep it on the Hush

Baby, I need you to keep what I'm about to tell you to yourself and not tell anybody. It's strictly confidential. I must admit, I want to get in between your split and do something different and explicit that's potentially monumental.

Seducing you subliminally from your mental, in ways that will cause your thought process to not process this sexual progress and shatter. Baby, I'm not less than the best, I know I can give you hot sex to make you climb not just the walls, but even up and down a ladder.

It doesn't even matter if it's dry; I can make it wetter than the seven seas when I get down to please on my knees with ease. They call me the Lick 'em Low Lover because I can please like no other while raising your body temperature to a hundred and three degrees.

Baby, you have no choice but to come and sleep with me, because my swagger and walk is way better than my chit chatter and talk. My bite's more vicious than my bark and I can sex you in a way to leave your body sensually lifeless to be outlined in chalk.

Making you want to stalk me like a sexual predator, starving hawk after climbing my meat stalk to the greatest high heights of sexual pleasure. I don't stand around like a pedestrian; I'm the only male lesbian that performs better in the bedroom than any thespian who can give you a continual eruption beyond any measure.

My sexual seduction is an inconspicuous treasure not known of, or have not been seen in the public eyes. My body movement dictates your movement, so there are concealed strings opening up your legs as if they were a puppet's thighs.

Then entering you, forcing you to moan and groan like a trumpet cries, as you try to adjust to my instrument's size and strength. Causing you to finally just relax and loosen up as your lips grasps the shaft and glides the length.

I'm giving what you want; flesh to flesh, wet with sweat as we kiss and caress, stroking harder and faster. And it now seems as if I'm possessed from your gentle tenderness, so I'm now the sex slave and you're the notorious master.

And your every wish is my command. I'll supply for every demand. I'll work out that wet muscle till your legs tremble, wobble, fade and fall to the point at which you just lay there and can't even stand.

Making you call me the man that served you up well who Angela Bassett couldn't even find when she was waiting to exhale. I'm the reason Tina stayed with Ike and the reason that Brandi Webb, from A Thin Line between Love and Hate, had a fight with herself and went to jail. I am that good looking, big meat slinging, tongue-twisting, good fucking black male that makes you yell.

But I don't play kiss and tell because whatever you tell your friends, they might want to find out for themselves if what you and I do is true. That's why we have to keep it to ourselves every time we get together and screw.

Baby, I let it do what it do till the deed is done and I do it till it's done well. And even if the odds are stacked up against me, I got the eye of the tiger like Rocky and the fight of a lion, so I will prevail.

Sometimes I just can't help myself. I'm a misfit when I twist it around then stick it and lick it. And you'll never have to nit-pick because I never hit quick, I got enough love to savor that's definite and so exquisite every moment, you'll never deny the fact that you want it and miss it.

I just need you to admit it. You must love it when I lick your inner thigh while reaching up high to tease your nipples with pleasure in your eyes. Then I lift you off your feet to join us complete while you throw your head back so sweet as you moan your silent cries to the skies.

And it ain't no surprise; even vegetarians can appreciate this good prime USDA government certified rare meat. Lord knows every time I lie in the bed it grows like Pinocchio's nose and gets anxious to lie within the deep wet cushions of its hot and damp hair seat.

And nobody will ever be able to compare me to any other because no other brother can display or even speak about the excellent performance that I always give. But remember, keep it on the hush; because we wouldn't want any of your friends to try to find out if the words I speak are really real.

Reading is Fundamental

Looking at Grandfather's arthritic hands rotate endlessly into eternity, the moments slowly passed as his arms became outstretched like an active athlete at a track meet toward the Roman numeral twelve. The Greek goddess Artemis was showing out and outdoing herself as the moon lay vibrantly held on an archaic canvass of silent sensuality and seemed as if the violet cool colors were fitted and molded to soothe others with an illustrious weld.

The sweet smells of burning Amber Romance candles rebelled the impurities in the crisp breeze as she sat on her patio with a with a fleece blanket over her chest and knees as glass number five of Moscato D'asti sat impatiently half empty at her side. The Art of Noise's Moments of Love was on repeat as wide flames on the oak raged with pride and tried their best to guide their way to revive and coincide with her flesh and provide heat so any stressed goose bumps wouldn't survive.

Her cellphone then suddenly came alive. "Hello," she answered in a sexy and sensual girl 6 operator voice. His was low, deep, semi-raspy and hoarse. "What's goin' on, Janet? I can no longer stand it. You're comin' with me tonight to another planet in my Rolls Royce, so don't fight my choice to show you delight to make you moist."

"Mmmm," she replied, nonchalantly as she sighed, "baby, as good as it sounds, getttin' high, and as much as I wouldn't mind for you to hoist and pound this round ass, I'll have to pass on the sexual healing because I'm busy this evening." He didn't even have to question what she was revealing because he already knew what the deal was and she had no reason to be deceiving.

She then quickly decided that she knew her thoughts were about to be leaving, so she disregarded the text message from unfamiliar numbers that were shown she was receiving and turned the ringer off on her phone. There would be no more interruptions or frivolous discussions of irrelevance killing her vibe while she tried to hide at home, butt bald naked and alone, entranced with her attention undivided in her zone.

Damn, I wish I had a clone to deal with the extra foolishness keeping me from this book. The night has shown to be perfect for indulging in chapters of erotic creativeness from the exotic greatness of this young cat by the name of Ol' Skool. I can't remember the last time some cool young fool was able to make this old cougar's cat salivate from his mental state and physically drool from just envisioning the penetration sensation of his mule.

My goodness, I can still envision how he had me soaking wet on my stool in euphoric submission from pictures he'd masterfully generated from his poetic scriptures that should be displayed and hanging like paintings up in the Louvre. That night, I was hypnotized as I had begun to subliminally groove and was sensually moved to please myself along the side of his confessed convictions as if he was a guilty convict in court speaking for sport with something to prove.

... "This is your one and only instruction. I only demand that you close your eyes and allow me to consume your thought process with my hypnotic seduction to generate the sexual progress for your body and soul's abduction.

My purpose *is* the corruption and consumption of your intellectual…so I can manifest and disperse sexual impulses to travel to the farthest erotic cerebral cortex of your brain. I'm here to put you under a *psychological* hypnosis…to tickle and tease your thoughts in manipulative ways so that the diagnosis *will* explain that you have symptoms of a sensual psychosis that proves you've been sexually driven insane.

Baby, my hypnotic tongue's dialog contains subliminal messages to bend your mind through time…so every sexual nerve throughout your body and soul can relax and unwind. Forcing you to sit back and find every intimate thought in your consciousness…coercing you to act it out like an illustrious mime.

So, this is not a choice…just follow the smooth rhythm and rhyme of my voice because it *can* promote internal racing sensations to get you moist. My mission *is* to hoist and uplift your spirit so your soul can really feel it as your essence expressively echoes to rejoice"…

That was the night Janet had begun to finger herself through the silk laced G-string she wore. She closed her eyes and pictured herself and Ol' Skool frantically tearing each other's clothes off, fucking on the floor.

Impulsively, she had opened her eyes at the poetry club, perused the room with a sigh of relief, 'Good, no one has noticed me.' She wasn't even listening to Ol' Skool's words, but she was imagining and feeling them subconsciously.

She was too busy being wrapped up in the thought of being wrapped up in his embrace. She had continued to masturbate in place, feeling her wet clit restrict her fingers even more while retaining a sincere and subtle look on her face.

She unconsciously then traced the lining of her panties and slid her fingers underneath. Pushing her pelvis forward in search of his dick, clenching her jaws and sucking through her teeth.

Thinking to her herself, 'Girl, I know we are new to this.' Then she wet her fingers with her tongue, tasting the wet juices from her own uterus.

My body wouldn't let my hands move far or fast enough in lust. I just wanted to bust and let love gush and break free. Photographic images of pornographic scenes are now clouding my visions to a point at which my thoughts and feelings do not agree.

At that point, my mind took over and I moved over pulsating mountains to a wet dream. And between squeezed thighs thoughts became faintly unclean.

The closed lids made visions verging on the edge of obscene, distant in a mirage. Then my hands made an elegant descent into my tent of moisture and cream and began spinning everything together like mind blending a collage.

Fitting tightly like a wedding ring and sliding softly into second base, I felt my hands and my heart rate begin to race, rising up and again down to a splashing rhythm. Again, I can only imagine what a better sensation it would be to feel the depth and pressure from Ol' Skool's rock-hard prism.

She then felt a buzzing sensation and pulsation between her legs. Shaken from fantasy in her head, right as Ol' Skool was beginning to beg, her phone was a vibrating nuisance, inadvertently pleasing her juices, forcing her thighs to loosen and spread.

The flickering red and white was like a strip club's strobe light instead as the flashes enhanced the pitch black atmospheres. But, she just tossed it on the floor because it was an unfamiliar number, this was the time of slumber, and she was so not ready to open any door, even to chat with peers.

She just wanted to get her mind wrapped and back to steering in the direction of a sexual source that she had planned for some intellectual intercourse with the first volume of "Ol' Skool's Sex Tools." It was a book given to her a few weeks ago from the man himself, the best dude, after a short conversation she had with him on that *same night she had left a wet stool.*

That night, it was as if Ol' Skool was the next cool vision that had entered her thoughts and spoke to her to make her cream in her dreams.

... "As you lie nude, similar to hot cooked food, in the scattered darkness like a battered carcass in your living room in a slumber, I decided to put you under my spell in this cell with iniquitous whispers.

Making the vibrations from my tongue create sensations to get you sprung as it sensuously slithers through orgasmic zones throughout the pores of your skin tone while each and every one of your defense mechanisms becomes splintered and just withers.

Baby, the main reason I came hither in this season was for the infliction of premonitions to promote illusions of hope for the conclusions of ambitious body collisions. I'm here to make a strenuous incision to transform your psyche. In addition, since it's hard to not invite me in, it's my decision to complete the sin before the first intermissions begin and I fade into your visions.

So, with precision, I need you to use your women's intuition as I peruse and abuse your mind's division...for you to decipher the meaning of my existence. My persistence will overcome any resistance. And I require no assistance to fuel the fire of desire because I'm prepared to take you the distance with no subsistence.

Just know that, in this instance, I insist this will force you to orgasmically leak from your core and magically be yours for the taking. This is mental love-making. Something that's known to be sewn into minds to publicize its rhapsody and many variations to get you fantastically shaking."...

Damn, that fine specimen of a man knew just what to say on any day to make my oceanic bay able to tear up and spray from his tongue's vocal seduction. Just a few impure thoughts of him can really get my blood rushin'.

So, nothing will keep me from taking out the time to read his rhythm and rhyme. I just have to see what I've been missin' and what has other women tryin' to mention as being the subjects of some of the pieces that had their soul's cryin'. I can still hear that bitch's voice, rambling and lyin'...

... "Girl, I can still remember the first time I saw him standing across the room. And I admit it, I wanted to hit it. I wanted to feel the strength of his strong arms wrap around me soon.

It was something about his cool swagger that kept him flickering in my eyes like the flame from a candle. And my sexual appetite was growing hungry for him in ways that I felt I couldn't handle.

I just wanted to sample his lust for one night to see what he was working with. This man was mysterious, the strong silent type, and so sexy with lips I longed to kiss.

And let's not dismiss the natural charismatic ways he seemed to exude about himself as he walked that dignified walk that he walked so well. And I could tell his body had to be chiseled in stone from the way his clothes fit about his broad shoulders and creased between his manly chest, as if he was a mahogany advertisement in a magazine for sale.

The inside of me was yelling from the first moment I knew he was about to approach me in conversation. I just fell deep into the pits of his bedroom seductive dark eyes and was lost in my own mischievous contemplation.

Only sexual exploitations were the thoughts scavenging like savages about my mind. And I know it's improper and not lady-like, but who cares, I have needs, too and I needed this man on this night to be mine."...

By this time, one of Grandfather's old crippled hands had moved a couple tries and had managed to point east. Fifteen minutes had already passed as her glass was now three-quarters empty, but her feast for the sensation of mental stimulation had not even began at the least.

Then, after a few moments, she cracked the book open to its first poetic piece, she was instantly subdued and left intrigued and wet while her thoughts were being laid for sex between the sheets of each page. It was about her and the night he was on stage. The night that she couldn't control her inebriated and fascinated rage.

Her primal inhibitions were soon released from their intuitive cage as her glossy eyes surveyed each and every, somewhat cocky detail written. It was like she was the prey of a vampire when first bitten. She felt the warmth of his words like a campfire given to force the purring of her kitten.

..."Janet wanted to kiss his full lips as his tongue flipped and emerged from his mouth. She wondered if he could do the things he spoke about, using his tongue and if he really liked licking down south.

The octave of his voice was so seductive and hypnotic, her mind became completely consumed with him using his tongue. She had never spoken to him, but for this instant she was completely sprung. And after noticing the slight bulge in his jeans, wondered if he was really hung.

Suddenly, she noticed his words had won her over as she could feel the faucets between her legs open and the juices began to flow. So she slowly crossed her legs and shifted her position to tighten and clench her wet muscle in a way that hopefully no one would know.

As she continued imagining him eating her, she could feel the wetness pooling in her G-string. She then wondered if anyone could smell the sex sweat but guessed that the musk-mixed smells of the club, perfume, and cologne could conceal anything.

Just by the power of suggestion, he seemed to be stuffing her head with exotic and erotic fantasies as her thoughts floated and lingered. She bit her lower lip, as her hands became his, rubbing her thighs and stomach, inconspicuously pinching and rolling her hardened nipples between his fingers."…

That damn Ol' Skool really knows what goin' on some times! Yea, he made up a few lines, but there's no crime in embellishing the sublime. I guess it's his poetic license, intertwined.

It's amazing how he can enter minds and decipher and decode with inner rhymes combined with creating shivers in her spine to make a bitch orgasmically stand in line for the next line to be laid on the line while he lines out the previous line of wrinkled lines to be absorbed in line in the system like cocaine lines.

Man, I would love to run into him again…talking about he was speaking of me while conversing his piece. I didn't believe until now as I read these words he delicately placed before my face that were burning my soul like hot fish grease.

Grandfather must have fainted in the distance and was now vexed and laid to rest as time had now seemed to cease to exist. Janet was completely in a trance as her mind amorously danced the forbidden romance of her and Ol' Skool in the midst of a sultry mist in the middle of an oceanic abyss.

She then bit her bottom lip and allowed a sweet moan to escape with a lisp as she imagined his impressionistic kiss between her thighs. Her middle and index finger simultaneously and sporadically had begun to glide and coast inside, mischievously without her permission to vibe.

At that point, after a few long strides, she tried to turn to the next sheet of sweet incandescent words, but the pages were moving in herds, sticking together. Janet had not realized that she was alternating with the same hand she was playing with herself with to follow along with some of the letters.

"Mmmm, I'm wet enough to put out a fire in a slaughter mill or, better yet, require a water bill," she thought to herself, sitting in the still of night, imagining the size of his pickle's dill while he would whisper killing words of pleasure to her treasure. And to add to the evening collage of aromas, the engulfing scent of her stuff had rushed up as a pocket of air burst through the crevices of her blanket and united together with the weather.

At that moment, a small poetic letter, addressed to her had slipped out that she hadn't noticed because Ol' Skool's words had her feeling as if she was a savage fiend for some hot meat like rabid bitch dog in heat. And like thick sap from an oak tree, succulent honey had leaked from that bee's hive as her index, middle, and now ring finger had begun to dive and seep inside her pride and joy while Ol' Skool's book became her new hideaway toy with each verse on each sheet forcing her closer to an invigorating treat, an overwhelming skeet.

Soon, in her peripheral, she noticed the note that lay aside her feet.

... "Greetings and salutations, mystery woman of the night. Hopefully this poetic kite finds you in the right state of mind, continuously great and kind, and you would like to someday rewrite history with us both coexisting in the extracurricular delight.

And despite barely even knowing you, I would like to get to know you and invite you out for an evening of possibilities to come. Instantaneous, spontaneous fun, rather than dealing with the fallacy of this dry ass reality, I'd rather dance and romance you deep within wet dreams, so our perception of reality is never what it seems when you cream and scream under the midnight sun and all is said and done.

Baby, I am the smoking gun with more power in my lungs to blow a cool breeze to weaken knees and chill spines with my powerful potent persuasive patois. I can give you that pleasant feeling that's hard to define; that unexplainable je ne sais qois.

And I hope you won't think it too sinful as the movie, "Trois," but a mutual friend of ours, from St. Croix, delivered the pen stroke of your contact info by the bar window when your back was turned and you were picking up the tempo of your feet to leave the last time you were here. So I made sure I spotted you the next time with this note in my book, just in case I saw you and had a little fear to whisper the right words in your ear.

I just want to hold you near one night. So hopefully you'll give me a call so we can allow something new to take flight."...

Janet's mouth dropped and even her hot twat was shocked as she slowed her rock and her memory rolodex had begun to slow the sex and frantically scroll and poll the reason that his number seemed to look so familiar, like she'd seen it somewhere before. It was puzzling to her mind's core. Suddenly, like eggs, she scrambled in heat to find her phone that she had earlier thrown on the floor.

Not ready for what it had in store, she typed in her password, which was, "never odd or even" written backwards, and like an "avid diva" in Bermuda that had "a nut for a jar of tuna," she tried to remember the message's last words. Listening carefully and attentively to each cast verb, she thought to herself that this dude by the name of, Ol' Skool, really had nerves.

... "Well, hello there, mystery woman of the night. I was given your number from our mutual friend the last time we passed words when I kind of let it slip that I admired your ass curves, and like a rifleman ready to strike, I had you in my sights.

So, since I hadn't heard your voice since that night I figured I just try to see if you'd answer *my* call. I'll be hones*t with you. No disrespect of speaking of sex, but ever since you crossed my eyeballs, I've had visions of altered variations of missionary positions and pressing you up against the drywall.

I would love the chance to try all and everything I know to bring down your love and affections from a high fall of ecstasy and temptation. But, since I haven't heard from you, my only thoughts is that you don't want to feel that sensation.

Baby, I have no reason to lie, so you can take my words as the truth when I say that I've been waitin' for quite some time, hoping that my phone would ring and you would be on the other end. I long for your touch and the chance to send erotic impulses from the lips above and below your chin to the lips above and below your shins by wrapping my flesh around yours, compressing it against your skin.

Allowing your thighs to be a synagogue for my sins while your love becomes my salvation. I want to be with you, with no deviation.

But, anyway, I hope you can excuse the time, I just felt the need at this moment to commit the crime of dropping you a line to further my ambitions. Nonetheless, if being in a position under my submission is not part of your mission, I can understand your disposition and won't bother you anymore.

And I apologize for the simple misconception and false perception of reality I live in within my own head."...

Even Janet's secretions had begun to sensually boil deep within her as she listened to Ol' Skool's words play back. He wanted her and she loved his word choice and the ways he'd say that.

She then typed in the number from the note so impatiently and hard she thought the screen may crack with each number pressed. She instantly became stressed. On the inside, she screamed because there wasn't even a first ring, and she was now agitated with this test.

How can this motherfucker sit here and confess all this good shit from his manhood and have his phone cut off! As wet as I just got from the luscious words spoken from his mouth, now he got the nerve to inadvertently cause a drought!?!?!?

It's too damn hot and humid down south for games. And I was really thinking of maybe letting him do something nasty and insane, but since he wanna gas me up in my brain, he can kick rocks, just the same.

Stuck in a frustrated and funky mind frame, she decided to go ahead and continue the rhyme game by reading the text that she ignored earlier before she got lost in her own world. The first was from an old classmate she'd been friends with since the third grade by the name of Pearl.

... "I kno you ain't sleep. Girl, get yo butt up & get here to the spot. Lol. dat hot nigga, Ol' Skool, is here askin for u dat u was tlkn bout.

He said he would hit u up in a few a few minutes ago, but lost his phone when he got out his car. N e way, get yo ass down here b4 he go too far."...

Janet quickly replied to her friend's text. She waited. She waited some more. And next, she waited. Split seconds became split sessions of split lessons on how to not split time between fallacy and reality when desiring to do the splits sexually. 'Believe in the mind and the body will follow,' you would think she had learned that lecture from the last time she was moved intellectually.

And, by this time, Grandfather seemed to be revived, alive, into a memorable mime, posing in a retro-seventies disco stance. It was right around a few minutes before a quarter after half past the second hour after midnight forcing him to sing and vibe with his slow dance.

In addition to a crisp low glance that manifested and crawled cruelly upon her face, her overall demeanor changed grace into a melancholic melody of rhythm and blues only played in the downtrodden juke joints and hole-in-the-walls in the south. She never received another text from her friend that night. Pearl was out and about enjoying the company and words from Ol' Skool's mouth, and that thought made Janet internally scream and shout.

She knew his dialog's dictation and conversation had enough clout to win over any woman that was in his presence. She knew he could take a woman's grey mental deterioration about love, romance and intimacy and give it incandescence and convalescence.

Her mind drifted back to shifted incisions and body collisions of her and that man that had been clouding her thoughts. Her legs were lifted and her head was tilted, while his tongue was gifted the chance to taste what his persona, alone, had bought.

Suddenly, a knock on the door followed by an innocent cough and clearing of a throat had rocked her back into the confines of her own home. She started to keep quiet and act like she was either asleep or gone, but there were even flashing lights on her phone.

'*Ugghhh, why won't these people leave me alone,*' she thought to herself as she answered, "who is there?"

"Girl, it's me, Lil' P," a voice shouted, seeming to come from beneath the door with an echo, like from underneath a stair.

As soon as she swung the door open, Ol' Skool was standing, shark bait, there grinning from ear to ear to make a heart break, immaculate, in a freshly pressed, double-breasted white Sean Jean button-up shirt with delicious aromas cruising the air waves to hurt impurities and insecurities of any other odors that aren't allowed to coexist with the aura of him. Needless to say, even though she looked a hot mess, the chances of Ol' Skool getting invited into her den for a process of hot sex were not too slim.

Then, in an instant, from behind the dim light in the distant, Pearl popped up and asked if Janet had received her message that they were about to leave and come to her house. It was the other unfamiliar number and text she had disregarded earlier. Using her male friend's phone, she said that she would come by and bring Ol' Skool if she saw him somewhere out and about and willing to succumb to the deviation in routes.

Rehabilitation

Greetings and salutations. I know some of you may have seen me at Seductive Eroticisms' graduation, but I was soon sent back here to this station for sexual rehabilitation.

Hello, my name is Ol' Skool, and I was in direct violation of my extensive probation for being a recovering undercover over lover, under covers. I have always had an addiction and oral fixation for that loose muscle that, when seen in tight jeans, looks like a moose knuckle that any man would have an energy-juiced hustle to get right on over away from his own mother to try to discover.

I just love being another lover's lover under covers, especially when I see that little sucker pucker up, grin or pout, and then open its mouth to devour my steel pipe to make my sexual water spout.

But, before I take Nefertiti's long lost daughter out, I want to tell you about the last time I went into a relapsed shock. A time of pure euphoric bliss, which damn near made my knee*caps lock*, where I lost *control* of all inhibition and began to *shift* into position out of the *backspace* and *insert* my *space bar* into the *end* of her exotic *home,* inside that sweet-gapped-spot.

From the time I *enter*ed the room; *alt*ernate visions of her delicious treat-wrapped-hot and wet for me wouldn't *delete* themselves out of my head or even allow me to *escape* this sexual temple of doom. Now, don't get me wrong, bodily incision from various missionary positions was never the mission for going to her home under the light of a full moon, but great conversation went to a sexual deviation real soon.

She became my goddess Oshun as we sat there conversing in her living room about the good, the bad, and the ugly. After a while, from the direction I was laying, if this was western playing, I'd be Clint and have an Eastwood in my pants as I lay there on her legs, feeling so lovely, massaging her feet and calves while she caressed my temples and rubbed me.

And, suddenly, at this point in time, my mind was going nuts like two drained, non-zoo tamed, bamboo-maimed, kangaroo brains, and not even Lui Kang could have kicked or tried to shove me away from this lovely, tried-and-true dame, even if he induced pain to this used swain like tattooed names or a stomach flu slain. We became the new slang, each others 'boo thang,' and I wanted to enter her tomb's frame and make her poontang cream like Wu Tang to leave a drool stain on that couch and have her lost in the cushions like loose change.

Then unexpectedly, boom, bang, even déjà vu strained to review lame moments of intimacy while the candle was now a mere yellowish blue flame of infamy and the minutes flew strange like a boomerang as her moist womb rained, and it was now time for a room change. I moved vain as a Kung Fu crane or a true gang of bats that grew fangs for blue veins in the night like Bruce Wayne through plain darkness as I followed her like an animated carcass, suspended and swinging on her every word like a noose hangs or if you came to ever view plain necklaces on 2 Chains.

Now let me reiterate, to not misconstrue thangs, the shoes came off at the door, and while most would probably subdue game and pursue fame like a whore, it was never in the plans to do thangs that most fools blame on pass-through trains and hullabaloo grains or how some crews claim to be a victim of circumstance. I went there for the adult company, so no out-of-the-blue sprains or interrupting impromptu chains of events could dent or hurt-the-plans. We had good music and liquor to move us through the night and just *that* was worth-the-dance.

But, somehow I was birthed-the-chance to flirt-with-hands as we lie there in her bed underneath the sheets in our underwear. Soon, I became touchy feely under there. I sensuously kissed and nibbled on her neck promoting a thunder flare of emotion and her body's lotion to start coastin' as I guided her hand over to my hardened cucumber there, so she didn't have to question when or wonder where.

And as soon as she turned and gave me her sensuous bedroom slumber stare, she was my honey bear. I wanted to snatch off her panties the way primal hunters tear away at their kill at will, since I was lost and still in transition. She wanted to fight the feeling on this night revealing so many possibilities, but I was wishin' her to succumb to some of this good life of dealing that she may have been missin'.

Our transmission then shifted from stop to go, then fast to slow as we became entranced. Everything was intensified as we held hands, slow grooving while fighting this dance of forbidden romance.

I could feel her breath in hyperventilating pants as my fingers continued to tickle and tease while she stroked my pickle with ease, impressed by its size and strength. And, as she rubbed on my chest and abs while I applied molested grabs, she became more and more turned on and more into it as her fingers would glide the length.

I was as hard as prized cement and hypnotized within her eyes of sinful pride and grin because she now relinquished all distinguished inhibition and fell into position, surrendering to the shimmering trustful hands of lustful temptation. And for the sake of this exotic narration, let's just say this erotic stagnation was now as hot as chaotic cremation.

Between her legs became my salvation as she tamed the hunger of my starvation with her love and affection. And, at first breach of her moist peach she gasped for possession of her last breath with the concession of my erection.

Silently, she moaned. Quietly, she groaned. Vibrantly, she owned up the challenge as she had not so violently shown me that she was willing to let me play poker by allowing me to go all in. Our tongues ferociously met on a hot and humid battlefield between lips of a paused grin while I delightfully played with her perfectly small twins.

Then, suddenly, my back became clawed skin as velvety strokes from my tongue crippled her nipple, sending little shocks of ecstasy to capture the most iniquitous sensations of rapture sent to the brain. My movement was slowed and chopped as I screwed through the rain to entertain and I could cherish the details of each scene pictured in each frame.

She was the vicious, yet luxurious, mythological beast that reigned, so I had to pull out Excalibur to tame her in the midst of the scattered darkness. Intensely, I would slay her, servicing her with the goods like a waiter by continuing to completely fill and then empty my greater self in and out of her sexually-mastered compartment.

It was a duel of silhouettes and shadows and the both of us were determined to be the victor. I then leaned back, while still deep within her and shackled her right ankle in my right hand, as if to spin her, and she became the auctioned sex slave and I became Mister.

But, I didn't twist her. Instead, I went left; motioned myself around the right side of her luscious thigh while still in tremendous depth, dividing her sultry lips with pride. I was in overdrive. In her ear, I whispered and told her, "damn," as she whimpered and I lay on my shoulder to ram my hips and dive into her watery prize.

She just continued to take the punishment with silent cries, lying on her back side while I rocked her boat in her adventurous oceans in vigorous motions, forcing it to capsize. I just wanted to baptize myself in her essence. I just couldn't help myself in her presence. I made sure I didn't stroke with half stride so I felt forced to grab high and slap thighs.

It was far from nap time, and just as the way a crab tries to hold its prey with all its strength, I held her onto me, tightly and slightly bent, with a boa constrictor's coiling embrace. This was more than enough on my plate. A quick shift in hips and we were now in a spooning position while I made the decision to continue my stabbing fork and knife incision to bring about more traces of grace and contortion on her face.

Then, all of a sudden, she switched up the pace of the race in our distorted space, taking glorious initiative. She passionately backed up, pushed me back on my back and took back control, climbing on top of me like a saddle and straddled me in a way that seemed notoriously primitive.

Her actions were meritoriously indicative of sheer enthusiasm and an infatuation for me as she graciously rode the currents that charged and promoted her turbulent wet white water rapids flow. It was groovy, I allowed her to use me and seduce me as I navigated and mapped out the peninsula in her sea like Amerigo Vespucci to show her why Ricardo loved Lucy while she took control, grinding immensely and slow while looking like an illustrious work of art from Vincent van Gogh.

Not even Henry David Thoreau would have written any criticism about her glow because "it's not what you look at that matters, it's what you see." In her eyes, there was a primal and carnal rage in disguise of pure thrilling pleasure and ecstasy.

So right in the middle of her sexing me, generating the bed's squeak while I was deep inside her heated treat, I slid myself and this unique freak a few feet down the sleek sheets so my feet were planted firmly and neatly on the floor. I wanted her to feel her tides crash against the sands of the shore.

Now, vertically shifted, she was lifted and was able to experience how gifted I truly was. Suspended in the thin air, skin bare, I was deep in there committing the sin where I was standing as if I held an unruly grudge.

Even giving her a booty rub as she bounced up and down, forcing me in, then out like I was a pogo stick. Just like cold peanut butter, she was oh so thick. We were sweaty and cramped and wrapped together in the hot and humid weather like the balls on a hobo's dick

We could have posed for a photo stitch or a logo pic in any book that Kama Sutra had to advertize. I knew she was glad the size of my manhood was as nurturing as a canned good, but this was only a little over half the ride.

She was the reason I was addicted in my second book. My erection took initiative and now had a mind of its own and had decided to think of the thought to have her thrown back on the bed like a selective crook.

Then, with a possessive hook in my grips, replanting my feet with a dancing dip in my hips, and moved as if I was trying to rearrange furniture. She mutedly squealed from the feeling that felt surreal as her face became reanimated and contorted like a caricature.

Suddenly, everything came to a halt. Instinctively, I pulled my treasure slowly from her vault. I was in complete awe. I can't really express into words what I saw.

So I was followed the law of sexual intuition in this variation of a missionary position and we passionately kissed. It was every colloquialism that can be formulated for pure ecstatic euphoric bliss.

To this moment, I reminisce and won't dismiss that fact that this turned me on even more and made me want to bump and grind in bolder ways. There were thighs on my stomach and calves on my chest. So, yes as you can guess, it was my pleasure to please and hold the praise.

There were ankles by my ears and even heels on my shoulder blades as I drove the maze of her juicy labyrinth with ease. To be honest, I was glad

I was the superior man that I was to please because any other inferior man would have been buckled at the knees.

As a boss, I propelled and thrust my wood beneath layers of wet flesh like a master splinter. As the king of the jungle, knee deep, like my calf was in her, the lioness roared in release of that good-feeling pain while I was in her safari, peeping over the trees of her canopy, as if a giraffe was in her.

Effortlessly, I then stooped to regroup, kissing her inner thighs as I allowed my tongue to slide to taste her dessert like after dinner. Her sweet peach, I wanted to taste. Between her legs, I wanted my face. My throat began to salivate as I gazed at that hot space.

But, I erased my ambition and went in another direction. There was a more dynamic and vital need to continue to fill her with me and satisfy with my erection.

Feeling mighty and damn cocky in her middle section, I proceed to flip her over on all fours so I could ride like a horse jockey. Delivering more meat than teriyaki, she was as wet as Saki by a lake in Milwaukee while I dug my man in her love and fought like the hand in the glove of Rocky.

This was doggy style and what shocked me was the fact that we had gotten froggy-wild while I was jumping in and out of her shaved territory. That ass, I smacked. She threw it back. To hell with worry, it seemed as if we both wanted to have pride if we ever would decide to tell the story.

I wish you could have felt the glory as I suppressed the sensations by licking and biting her bottom lip until she noiselessly yelled it for me, exhausting definite pleasure with the hot air. This moment between the moments was all that mattered. Neither of us cared how we got there.

And, although not a lot care that it's not fair, if one finishes before the other, I made sure that my lover was quite pleased and that I let her know that I could keep going if I needed to suspend, seize and suppress my release. Yet, to my knowing expertise, I was already sure, but was just seeing if she wanted another cure of guarantees.

So, now the end was staring me in the eyes. As the electric energy surged to generate my orgasmic purge, my strength was no surprise as I had seemed to metamorphasize to have an out-of-body experience. I stroked harder and harder, then faster and faster as my heart pounded and pounded and raced and raced, something serious. I was delirious.

Then, suddenly at that point of no return, I pulled out and exploded on her back and cheeks. As a matter of fact, I think a little bit of it got in her hair and sheets.

Completely relaxed and empty, I then sluggishly moved through the darkness with my hands outreached to feel my way to the bathroom so I could retrieve a towel to clean up the skeet that was sprayed on her flesh.

And after the cleanup of that mess, we just laid there and went to sleep, holding each other in that stolen moment as if it was our last breath.

So, as you can probably guess, there is a need for me to be in this rehabilitation center. My name is Ol' Skool, and I'm a recovering undercover over lover, under covers. And since we all have the same problem, only y'all can help solve 'em with more erotic stories for me to live and discover.

About the Author

    I was born the first best thoughts of great sex, purposely, Howard McAfee; not an accident or an incident, but an instant significant infant from a little bit of nothing. I rested in my mother's belly for nine months and some change, while she went through nine months of change and endured that pain of stomach rumbling and pushing and shoving innocence into a world of sin that has no mercy for the weak. Then I was forced to begin my life in the twilight on 12-21-83, and live it right, awake, not sleep and become something.

    And ever since then, I tried to do something to leave a positive impact on every person's life I've ever came in contact with and touched in some way. Raised in Texas City, Texas by the bay, I was always a youngster trying to explore something different on any day to see how many talents I could show off and display.

    And though I constantly preferred to play and be the fool over school, I always managed to maintain my cool and do well, as far as grades are concerned. But I think I learned most of everything I know from the older folks I grew up around with; they churned my mind and showed me how nothing is ever given to you, everything in life has to be earned.

    And because of that, from an early age, the name Ol' Skool and other synonyms was burned into my brain for the fact that I had an older point of view than most of my peers. I preferred blues music over screwed music, poetry and Dolemite over any of the rap fights, and the way I talked, dressed and carried myself was beyond my years.

Even some of the older folks would clear it up for me and say that I've been here before, so that's how my alias came about. And without a doubt, I took up the name with pride when I started writing and my poetry began to sprout.

Believe it or not, I always thought that anything I wrote never had any clout; I thought the content was corny and was something no-one would ever want to read. So, I just would write and maybe tell them to a few over the phone, and throw most away because it would be something I would never need.

It wasn't until Dedrick Johnson took me to the Shadow Bar when I wanted and started to take poetry seriously. And a few years after that, a good friend of mine by the name of Reisha, took me to another reading and made me speak, which demolished the fear in me.

And ever since then I've been writing and speaking in various clubs throughout Houston and other places. And in between work and school with dedication, I've managed to put this book together with the help of God's graces.

Acknowledgements

Honestly, at this time in my life, with all the things that I've been through, it's kind of hard to acknowledge all the folks that have been an inspiration or have had a significant impact on my life or some of the pieces in this book. There are really too many to name. But to those that know me personally, know that I deeply appreciate who you are to me. Some have seen me rise and fall, when I was low or tall, yet have never judged, but continued to be a part of my support system. Friends have become family. Family have become strangers. Enemies are now friends. You have all aided and help shaped me into becoming the man I am over time. Some of these poems date back over fifteen years. I just thank God that I'm able to still share my gifts effectively to those who truly appreciate and enjoy it. What's become my breath of fresh air, my release, has also become the oxygen for others to enjoy and be able to fill their lungs with also. So, to all those I, or my words, have ever touched, in any way, form or fashion, good or bad, this is for you. Thank you.

www.ingramcontent.com/pod-product-compliance
Lightning Source LLC
Chambersburg PA
CBHW051049160426
43193CB00010B/1124